Crosscurrents / Modern Critiques / New Series

Edited by Matthew J. Bruccoli

Margaret Drabble
Existing Within Structures

Mary Hurley Moran

Southern Illinois University Press
Carbondale and Edwardsville

Library of Congress Cataloging in Publication Data

Moran, Mary Hurley, 1947–
    Margaret Drabble, existing within structures.

    (Crosscurrents/modern critiques. New series)
    Bibliography: p.
    Includes index.
    1. Drabble, Margaret, 1939–   —Criticism and interpretation.
I. Title. II. Series
PR6054.R25Z76 1983   823'.914   83-332
ISBN 0-8093-1080-5

For Mike and Alison
and for My Parents,
Mary and Bill Hurley

Contents

Acknowledgments

Acknowledgment is made to Alfred A. Knopf, Inc. for permission to quote from the copyrighted works of Margaret Drabble.

Acknowledgment is made to the following for permission to reprint previously published material: William Morrow & Company: Excerpts from Margaret Drabble's *A Summer Bird-Cage, The Garrick Year, The Millstone,* and *Jerusalem the Golden*; The University of Wisconsin Press: Excerpts from Nancy S. Hardin, "An Interview with Margaret Drabble," *Contemporary Literature*, 14 (1973), 273–95; The Paris Review, Inc.: Excerpts from Barbara Milton, "Margaret Drabble: The Art of Fiction LXX," *Paris Review*, No. 74 (1978), pp. 40–65.

I wish to thank Margaret Drabble for permission to quote from her unpublished letter to Monica Lauritzen Manheimer, and the latter for sending me a copy of this letter as well as the transcript of her interview with Drabble.

I also wish to thank Hugh Witemeyer, Morris Eaves, and, in particular, Mary Power, of the University of New Mexico, for their advice, criticism, and support with regard to the writing of this study.

Margaret Drabble

Existing Within Structures

1

Introduction

At the age of forty-two, Margaret Drabble has already produced
nine novels and established herself as one of Britain's major living
novelists. Her recent appointment to the editorship of the revised
Oxford Companion to English Literature indicates her growing importance in English letters. And yet this talented writer, who has been
hailed as a twentieth-century George Eliot[1] and compared favorably
with Dickens,[2] had planned on an acting, not a literary, career. Although an excellent student of literature—she read English at Cambridge, graduating with a double-first in 1960—she spent her undergraduate years acting in university productions, and upon
graduation joined the Royal Shakespeare Company with her husband, Clive Swift, whom she had married just after leaving Cambridge. But fate, in the form of an early pregnancy, changed the
course of Drabble's career: her condition radically curtailed the
range of roles available to her, and consequently, sitting backstage as
an understudy, she turned her energies to writing a novel. This
book—*A Summer Bird-Cage*, published in 1962—was so well received
by the critics, and Drabble found writing to be so much more com-
patible with motherhood, that she dropped her plans for acting and
stuck with her new-found career.

It is not surprising, however, that Drabble took up writing so
easily, for she comes from a literary, intellectual background. Born
in Sheffield in 1939, she was the second of four children (three girls
and a boy) of a schoolteacher mother and a judge father, who en-
couraged the children to develop their literary interests. Drabble's
sister, who goes by the name A. S. Byatt, became a writer and scholar,[3] and since his retirement her father has devoted his time to
writing novels. Drabble's own literary talents have found expression
in a large outpouring of nonfictional works as well as her better

known fictional ones. The former include: a scholarly book on Wordsworth (*Wordsworth*, 1966); an essay on Virginia Woolf ("Virginia Woolf: A Personal Debt," 1973); an essay on the Brontës ("The Writer as Recluse: The Theme of Solitude in the Works of the Brontës," 1974); a biography of Arnold Bennett (*Arnold Bennett*, 1974); a collected edition of Jane Austen's unfinished and unpublished novels (*Lady Susan, The Watsons, Sanditon*, 1974); an edition of critical essays on Hardy (*The Genius of Thomas Hardy*, 1976), which includes an essay of her own ("Hardy and the Natural World"); a children's book about the Victorian Age (*For Queen and Country: Britain in the Victorian Age*, 1979); and a book-length study of the relationship between the classical English writers and their native landscape (*A Writer's Britain: Landscape in Literature*, 1979). Furthermore, she has done a good bit of journalism, publishing articles in the major London newspapers, the *New York Times*, and a variety of women's magazines.

However, it is novel writing that Drabble considers her primary vocation. She is always at work on a novel, with the result that she publishes one on an average of every two or three years. This dedication to the craft of fiction has been reflected in a steady growth in both her subject matter and technique over the past two decades. Her first five novels, which she wrote while a housebound young mother in her twenties, are limited in scope to her own particular concerns at that time: pregnancy, childbirth, the emotions of motherhood, and the role conflicts educated young women of the 1960s were subject to. The first three—*A Summer Bird-Cage* (1962), *The Garrick Year* (1964), and *The Millstone* (1965)[4]—are narrated in the first person by the protagonist, in a subjective, personal tone. Although in her fourth novel, *Jerusalem the Golden* (1967), she employs third-person point of view and in her fifth, *The Waterfall* (1969), alternates between third person and first person, she is still primarily looking through the eyes of the female protagonists.

But beginning with her sixth novel, *The Needle's Eye* (1972), Drabble departs from her usual techniques and subjects, no longer limiting her canvas to a female protagonist and her perceptions of the world. In *The Needle's Eye* she presents a male as well as a female protagonist; in *The Realms of Gold* (1975), although Frances Wingate is the central character, the thought-processes of several others, including males, are also probed; in *The Ice Age* (1977) the protagonist is a man; and in *The Middle Ground* (1980), as in *The Realms of Gold*, Drabble explores the consciousnesses of the major male characters.

Her handling of third-person point of view becomes more deft in these novels, after an initial unsuccessful attempt in *Jerusalem the Golden*, where she slides uneasily between identification with the protagonist and ironic detachment from her. The critic Joan Manheimer's remark about this development in Drabble is apt: "*The Needle's Eye* reveals the fruits of 'the long apprenticeship.' In it, Drabble explores the recesses of an interesting variety of figures and modulates between interior and exterior perspectives with a flexibility reminiscent of George Eliot."[5]

Her subject matter also widens with her sixth novel. The settings, which in the early books are constricted in geographical locale and range of characters, begin to encompass larger areas and a wider variety of people. *The Needle's Eye* ranges over many sections of London, from the shabby working-class neighborhood in the north where Rose Vassiliou lives to the fashionable Hampstead neighborhood of Simon Camish. *The Realms of Gold* portrays not only the protagonist's London environment, but also her rural ancestral home in northern England and the African countries where she lectures and does field work. *The Ice Age*, a major subject of which is the economic and political difficulties of contemporary Britain, provides an Olympian perspective of the entire country and contains scenes set in a fictitious Balkan state. And although the major action of *The Middle Ground* occurs in London, there is an international cast of characters, hailing from such places as Lebanon, Iraq, continental Europe, and the United States.

Another indication of Drabble's growth as a novelist is the widening of the protagonists' occupations and interests. In the first five novels the major characters' professions or inclinations are literary, while in *The Needle's Eye* Simon Camish is a Trades Union lawyer, in *The Realms of Gold* Frances Wingate is an archaeologist, Karel Schmidt an historian, and David Ollerenshaw a geologist, and in *The Ice Age* Anthony Keating is a real estate developer. Although in *The Middle Ground* Drabble again creates a protagonist of a literary bent, Kate Armstrong's field is journalism, a career which brings her into contact with many types of people and occupations. This branching out in her later novels allows Drabble to examine the various social, political, economic, and legal issues which affect and inform the existences of contemporary people. Her fiction thus provides a holistic picture of society, another way in which this author resembles George Eliot.

The comparisons with Eliot please Drabble, for she has placed herself squarely in the mainstream tradition of the British novel. An avowed realist, she aims for both physical and psychological verisimiltude, believing that life is a "mixture of emotional experiences and self-analysis and going to the post office."[6] In a 1967 interview she stated her position: "I don't want to write an experimental novel to be read by people in fifty years, who will say, ah, well, yes, she foresaw what was coming. I'm just not interested. I'd rather be at the end of a dying tradition, which I admire, than at the beginning of a tradition which I deplore."[7]

It was her aptitude for realistic portrayal that early on won Drabble a warm reception from reviewers. Again and again they praised her ability to write "very close to the grain of immediate contemporary life."[8] In addition, they pointed out her lucid, intelligent style, and many compared her with ranking contemporary novelists, predicting that she would develop into one of Britain's major writers. The *Times Literary Supplement* review of *The Garrick Year*, for instance, states, "It is not just the accuracy of the observations, the dialogue and the descriptions which are impressive but the feeling that here is a writer of real significance, using the English language with precision but without affectation, and shaping words and plot to a clear purpose. She has the cogency of an Iris Murdoch without the creamy symbolism."[9] And *Library Journal*, in its review of *The Millstone*, makes a similar judgment: "Miss Drabble is an author to watch, somewhat reminiscent of an uncomplicated Iris Murdoch."[10]

Her early novels also received attention because of the subject matter that Drabble was rapidly making her own: the situation of the educated, promising young woman who, upon marrying and having a baby, suddenly finds "her horizons shrunk to diaper size."[11] Although Drabble did not invent this theme, her treatment of it was considered superior: "This dog-eared problem, this subject of the self-pitying outbursts of Doris Lessing and the corruscating complaints of Simone de Beauvoir, is treated here as freshly as if it had just come up for the first time."[12]

It was no doubt Drabble's sensitive presentation of this theme that gained her a largely female readership for her early novels. But with the publication of *The Needle's Eye* her reputation began to change. With this novel, which contains a major male character and treats issues other than the exclusively female, reviewers began to discuss the author's more universal, moral concerns and argue that the label "women's novelist" did not really apply to Drabble. Anthony Thwaite, reviewing the novel for the *New Statesman*, declares, "But what is her central concern? From the way Margaret Drabble's novels have been written about in the past, one takes it that she is supposed to deal chiefly—and to the point of obsession—with the difficulties of being a woman . . . *The Needle's Eye* shows more clearly than ever before that this is inaccurate and unjust. She is not concerned with the difficulties of being a woman but with the difficulties of being good. And *The Needle's Eye* is the best novel on this rarely dealt-with subject since *Middlemarch*."[13]

Beginning with *The Needle's Eye* Drabble's novels, while still touching on certain female concerns, have focused more on the problems, which confront both men and women, of living in the bewildering contemporary world. Consequently, her readership appears to be widening and including more and more males. Her early novels were best-sellers in England, but she did not begin to catch on in the United States until the mid-seventies, when popular American magazines started regularly reviewing her books. Today Drabble is well known in both countries, her novels frequently appearing on college syllabuses for both women's literature and contemporary fiction courses. Her books have been reprinted in Penguin, Signet, and Popular Library paperback editions. According to the editor of Weidenfeld and Nicolson, Drabble's British publisher, sales of her books are among the highest for living British novelists, her most recent novel, *The Middle Ground*, having sold over 15,000 copies in England.[14]

Because Drabble's typical protagonist is an intelligent, independent-minded woman, much of the scholarly writing about her fiction has been done by feminist critics. However, there is a range of opinion on the question of Drabble's own attitude toward feminist issues. While her novels delineate the bitterness and sense of injustice felt by many women living in a patriarchal society, they at the same time dwell on the joys of motherhood, family life, and romantic love. This ambivalence on Drabble's part opens her novels to a variety of interpretations regarding their message about contemporary women's situation.

Most of the critics note that Drabble's women are fatalistic about their lives, usually succumbing, though sometimes bitterly or confusedly, to patriarchal society's role expectations. Virginia K. Beards, in "Margaret Drabble: Novels of a Cautious Feminist" (1973), argues that Drabble's motive for presenting this deterministic picture is to attack patriarchal society indirectly by exposing its pernicious conditioning of women. Thus, she sees Drabble's novels as politically didactic: "The conversion of the sexual protest into novels is what makes her interesting. The choices of artist over activist and imitation over frontal attack allow a subtlety and sensitivity that politics frequently precludes."[15]

Although Beards' analysis of the power patriarchal society has over Drabble's women is perceptive, this critic fails to note the author's very real attraction to certain traditional aspects of the female role. Elaine Showalter comes closer to the truth when she remarks, in *A Literature of Their Own: British Women Novelists from Brontë to Lessing* (1977), "Of all the contemporary English women novelists, Margaret Drabble is the most ardent traditionalist."[16] She observes that for "Drabble's heroines, at least up to Rose Vassiliou in *The Needle's Eye* (1972), there is a kind of peace in the acknowledgment of, and submission to, female limitation,"[17] and "a room of one's own is usually a place to have a baby."[18] Both Showalter and Marion Vlastos Libby, another feminist critic, are impatient with Drabble's traditionalist tendencies, but they see *The Needle's Eye* as marking a new stage in the growth of the author's feminist consciousness. Libby, in "Fate and Feminism in the Novels of Margaret Drabble" (1975), points out that Rose Vassiliou is allowed greater freedom than the earlier heroines: "[her] beauty and strength consist precisely in a struggle against the preordained circumstances of her life."[19] And Showalter observes that in this novel "graceful resignation to feminine destiny, to the curse of Eve, has come to seem much more masochistic and despairing."[20] She concludes, "[Drabble's] work is the record of a feminine consciousness expanding and maturing. In some respects she has been clinging to a tradition she has outgrown. *The Needle's Eye* is evidently the end of a prolonged phase in Drabble's writing; perhaps she will not allow herself more freedom, more protest."[21]

Joan Manheimer, in "Margaret Drabble and the Journey to the Self" (1978), regards *The Waterfall* as the turning point in Drabble's feminist development. She agrees with other critics that the early protagonists are not autonomous individuals and shows that their identities are fluid. While this problem is in good part due to their identities' being subsumed under their husbands' and lovers', Manheimer points out that a "close examination of the novel tradition suggests, however, an equal and perhaps more dangerous threat to female autonomy levelled by other women. Women in the novel frequently suffer a division of the world; they often are paired in an unrelenting complementarity which insists that whatever quality one possesses, the other, by necessity, lacks."²² Tracing this tradition through *Pride and Prejudice, Vanity Fair, Middlemarch,* and other nineteenth-century novels, she shows that it has been inherited by twentieth-century writers, for example, Doris Lessing, who, in *The Golden Notebook,* falls back on it in her pairing of Anna and Molly. This pattern is also found in Drabble's early novels: Sarah Bennett (*Bird-Cage*), Clara Maugham (*Jerusalem*), and Jane Gray (*Waterfall*) each depend on a female inverse double for identity: Sarah on her sister, Louise; Clara at first on her mother and later on her new friend Clelia Denham; and Jane on her cousin Lucy. But, Manheimer argues, Drabble is finally able to free herself from this dependence and create autonomous women: Jane eventually dissolves her symbiotic bond with Lucy and discovers her own identity, and Rose Vassilious is "powerfully centered within herself."²³ Manheimer's assessment of Drabble's development echoes Showalter's when she concludes that the creation of a heroine like Rose is an "index of Drabble's maturity."²⁴

But it is *The Realms of Gold*, Drabble's seventh novel, that is usually regarded as the culmination of her feminist development. In this book Frances Wingate, the protagonist, possesses the will and determination to shape her life that Rose only tentatively and intermittently grasps. In many ways a "super-woman," Frances manages a successful, high-powered career as well as the single-handed raising of her four children. Because of these features, many feminist readers and critics applaud this novel as Drabble's best and most mature. Carey Kaplan, for example, in "A Vision of Power in Margaret Drabble's *The Realms of Gold*" (1979), argues that by means of pervasive uterine imagery Drabble demonstrates the creative ability, both physical and imaginative, peculiar to women. Explaining that "the essence of uterine imagery [is] an enclosure in which what is potential becomes actual, in which the past merges with the present to create the future, in which harmony is wrought out of chaos," she points out that *The Realms of Gold* is filled with both actual and figurative holes awaiting this kind of transformation.²⁵ Whereas other characters, particularly Frances' depressed nephew Stephen, see only emptiness or futility in these voids, Frances can create things out of them—"a book, a child, a city, a life, a past."²⁶ The novel is, then, according to Kaplan, a celebration of female power.

Judy Little, in "Humor and the Female Quest: Margaret Drabble's *The Realms of Gold*" (1978), locates another uniquely female motif in this novel. Contending that female experience belies Northrop

Frye's quest myth, she suggests that one which more accurately reflects the shape of this experience is the Persephone-Demeter myth. This is an archetype for the plot of many comic novels about women, she argues, claiming that *The Realms of Gold* provides an excellent illustration. This novel is comic in both the structural sense—it has a happy ending—and the ordinary sense—it contains much humor. According to Little, women's humor depends on "how far a woman has come in the process of freeing herself from psychological, domestic, and social restrictions."[27] In *The Realms of Gold* both Frances and her young cousin, Janet Bird, have senses of humor, but these differ according to their relative degrees of freedom and liberation. The two women represent two different stages in the female quest. Janet is the Persephone figure at the beginning of the quest, in the descent-into-the-underworld stage. She is "barely awake; her sense of humor is defensive, oblique, and intermittent."[28] Frances represents a "later, more happy stage of the same quest."[29] She is both Demeter, who rescues Persephone, and the ascended Persephone. She has godlike power and energy; her humor is happier and more irreverent than Janet's. These equations are further borne out by the imagery patterns. Janet is associated with cataclysms, volcanoes, molten wax; such imagery implies a buried, underworld existence. Frances is associated with excavation imagery, and this implies her function as rescuer of Janet and others. Little concludes that the humor in this novel "belongs both to protest and to celebration."[30] Like Kaplan, she finds the book to be about women's power and to embody, in the person of Frances, a hope for the future: "Laughter, in the Demetrian myth, indicates the end of despair and the beginning of health and courage."[31]

Drabble herself has resisted the label "women's novelist" and expressed some annoyance with the feminist criticism of her fiction.[32] "I'm a feminist only when I have certain accusations flung at me," she has declared. "But I don't think I write particularly for women. I just happen to be one."[33] She has also contended, "None of my books is about feminism."[34] She chose a male protagonist for *The Ice Age* because she was "fed up with women—slightly."[35] Some of these remarks were undoubtedly made lightly, for she does display many feminist attitudes: she has deplored the unequal treatment of women,[36] praised Virginia Woolf for her sensitive portrayal of the difficulties encountered by the woman who wants a career,[37] and conducted her own life in a manner most would call liberated.[38] In short, she is a moderate—or, to use Virginia Beards' term, cautious—feminist, distancing herself from the radical and militant branches of the movement because she finds their reasoning and rhetoric destructive.[39]

Ironically, although Frances Wingate is considered by feminist readers to be a model of the liberated woman, Drabble's own comments indicate that the author regards her as not so much an example of feminist achievement as simply a lucky person. Drabble claims to have stacked the decks in favor of Frances: "the characters [in *The Realms of Gold*] do indeed appear to behave with much more freedom and spontaneity [than the characters in *The Needle's Eye*]. And also they leave their respective husbands and wives and remarry. But this appearance of freedom and happiness can only be achieved by a lot of tricks in the plot, and by refusing to allow the other spouses to come very clearly into focus."[40]

Writing to a friend before the publication of *The Realms of Gold*, she said, "My next book is in a sense an answer to *The Needle's Eye*. It is called *The Realms of Gold*, and it ends happily for all, particularly for my very lucky archaeologist heroine. . . . But it has a certain flippancy, a certain selfishness even—Everybody remarries happily in the last chapter. An element of the fairy story at work?"[41]

Furthermore, some of Frances Wingate's remarks imply a far from feminist outlook; for example, Frances is "rather confused about Freud's views of women. While not quite able to accept the theory of penis envy, she was more and more convinced that what every woman wanted was a man, and that what every man wanted was a woman, and that if they didn't want that they ought to, and that the only possibility of happiness and harmlessness on earth was to be found where Freud would have us find them, and that there was no way out of this" (*Realms*, p. 185).

Kate Armstrong, the protagonist of *The Middle Ground*, holds a similarly ambivalent attitude toward feminism. Like Frances, she lives an outwardly liberated life while inwardly still subject to certain unliberated female attitudes: despite a failed marriage and a series of soured heterosexual relationships, she continues to long for romantic love, and she finds her greatest fulfillment and sense of purpose in the maternal role. Although she has always been an outspoken feminist, in middle age Kate suddenly becomes cynical about the direction the women's movement is taking, wondering whether feminism is still a good cause.[42] By means of a sharply satirical scene in which the protagonist spars with a strident American feminist, Drabble expresses her distaste for the angry rhetoric adopted by the movement in the States. And thinly-veiled allusions to Marilyn French's *The Women's Room* imply the author's criticism of the commercial exploitation of the movement by the new breed of feminist novelists.

Despite Drabble's irritation with feminist critics and her desire to shed the label "women's novelist," many readers and critics persist in looking for feminist messages in her works. Indeed, the thesis of Ellen Cronan Rose's recent study of Drabble, *The Novels of Margaret Drabble: Equivocal Figures* (1980), is that the author *ought* to be holding up feminist models although she is not doing so. Rose feels that Margaret Drabble's early novels raised questions about women's choices that ought to be answered in her later novels. In *A Summer Bird-Cage* Sarah longs to have her cake and eat it too—to have both a career and marriage, both intellectual and emotional fulfillment— but she knows that for women of her generation such a future is not possible. The next few novels illustrate the truth of this view, portraying women who have had to settle for a narrow, one-sided existence. But with *The Waterfall*, Rose feels, Drabble finally creates a woman who manages to achieve integrity and autonomy.[43] Given this development, Rose would have Drabble continue in a feminist direction, creating female protagonists who can serve as models for contemporary women. But Drabble retreats from this goal. In *The Needle's Eye* she does not finally allow Rose Vassiliou to break free of patriarchal institutions, as this character has verged on doing. In *The Realms of Gold* she creates a woman whose solution to living in a patriarchal society is personal rather than political and so of no help to women readers.[44] And in *The Ice Age* she refuses to develop the character of Alison Murray, a potential feminist example, concentrating instead on Anthony Keating and his embracing of patriarchal ideals.

Ellen Rose sees a "hidden agenda of women's liberation"[45] in Drabble's novels. By allowing characters like Rose Vassiliou to be on the verge of breaking free of patriarchal society's strictures and by creating characters like Emily Offenbach (*Needle's Eye*) and Alison Murray, who if given freer reign could prove subversive to the novels' male-dominated societies, Drabble implies an unconscious desire to make a radical feminist statement. Rose would like her to stop running away from this vision and to come out with strong feminist messages. She concludes her study with a plea to Drabble to make her next book "an unequivocally feminist blueprint."[46]

Ellen Rose's scholarship is impeccable and her analyses of the novels are in many ways brilliant; but she is concentrating on what *could be* in Drabble's fiction and not on what is there. She views Drabble's conservative impulses as perverse denials of her true, feminist vision rather than as authentic aspects of the author's philosophy. There are many critics, however, who regard Drabble's conservatism as the heart of her vision. François Bonfond, for example, argues that Drabble's characters who accept the workings of fate achieve a greater wisdom and a deeper happiness than those who do not. He argues that Emma Evans' *(Garrick Year)* and Rosamund Stacey's *(Millstone)* ultimate renouncing of "selfish free will"[47] and embracing of the role of mother is presented as a positive act, whereas Sarah Bennett and Clara Maugham, still caught up in youthful "aimlessness and immature dreams,"[48] are to be regarded as undeveloped.

Nancy S. Hardin, in "Drabble's *The Millstone*: A Fable for Our Times" (1973), discovers a similar theme in *The Millstone*. She argues that acceptance of fate, which for Rosamund takes the form of an unwanted pregnancy, is responsible for the protagonist's deepening of character and attainment of wisdom. Prior to this experience, Rosamund's intellectual, theoretical side was vigorously developed, but her emotional side was neglected because she arranged her life to avoid intimate involvement with others. However, her belief in free will and her theoretical approach to living disintegrate when the emotions and instincts of motherhood emerge. Living for another means no longer having complete control over one's life. This submission to fate provides Rosamund with a kind of knowledge she previously lacked, intellectually brilliant though she was—knowledge regarding what it means to be a human being. Hardin points out, "As a result of her millstone, she regains the lost dimension of depth in her own life. She learns to love. Given who she is and the basic honesty of her confrontations with the world, she paradoxically opens for herself the possibilities of freedom. As Camus' Sisyphus finds joy within the confinements of his existence, so does Rosamund when she accepts the 'no choice' of her predicament."[49]

Intriguingly, in an article published several years before her book and before her own personal feminist revolution, Ellen Rose praises Drabble for showing that wisdom and happiness lie in acceptance of the contingencies and limitations of existence. In "Margaret Drabble: Surviving the Future" (1973), she points out that all of Drabble's heroines display a longing to escape into dreamworlds of felicity and perfection which they created in childhood. Each of the protagonists wrestles with the discrepancy between this ideal and reality. Drabble's conclusion, Rose argues, appears to be that the ideal can be achieved only at great expense—usually, the forfeiting of one's humanity, as evidenced by Clara Maugham, who through sheer will achieves her ideal but fails to develop compassion and love. True maturity and a more profound happiness are to be found in renouncing dreams and settling for "messy reality."[50] Rose sees a similarity between Drabble's philosophy and Wordsworth's: both the novelist and the poet feel that the visions of childhood cannot be sustained in adulthood, but that the loss of these is compensated for by the attainment of a philosophical happiness and a deeper understanding of humanity.[51]

The first book published on Drabble, Valerie Grosvenor Myer's *Margaret Drabble: Puritanism and Permissiveness* (1974), argues that "Margaret Drabble's continuing theme is a reconsideration and revaluation of the English puritan tradition. She has recognised that this strain, though popularly denied, is still very much with us and has left us an inheritance of guilt and anxiety. . . . The extended analysis of the puritan inheritance, played out in all her leading characters, is her characteristic and unique contribution to the contemporary novel."[52] Myer's study consists in part of a demonstration of how the puritan legacy influences the psychology and behavior of each of the major, as well as some of the minor, characters. This aspect of her work is important, for Drabble's protagonists are unusually obsessed with guilt, grace, salvation, and providence. However, Myer goes on to argue that the protagonists' puritan consciences are at odds with their true natures, which if unimpeded would direct them toward love, community, and spontaneous joy. Drabble, Myer says, demonstrates in her characters' conflicts and development that a puritan streak must be reconciled with an instinct for enjoyment. All Drabble's characters resolve this conflict, though with varying degrees of success, and are eventually able to love and involve themselves with others.

Patricia Sharpe, in "On First Looking into *The Realms of Gold*" (1977), disagrees with Myer's perception that the protagonists become healthy, happy, and socially involved by the end of the novels. Sharpe accurately points out that while they do learn to live according to their true natures, these natures do not always lead them to the kind of healthy adjustment Myer would have. Rather, some characters, for example Stephen Ollerenshaw, are by nature psychologically unhealthy. But Drabble, who appreciates the uniqueness and otherness of individuals, feels it is good for one to develop along the lines of one's true nature, no matter what it is like.[53]

The value of Myer's study is that she has drawn attention to Drabble's dark, at times almost Calvinistic, outlook; her mistake is to assume that Drabble is gradually shedding, or at least attempting to shed, this outlook in favor of a "healthier" one. In fact, Drabble's works suggest a deep emotional and philosophical attachment to the concepts of determinism and fatalism. In her response to Monica Manheimer's article, "The Search for Identity in Margaret Drabble's *The Needle's Eye*" (1975), Drabble expresses the core of her philosophy:

> Both Rose and Simon are, it is true, trapped inside their own personalities, but then, so is everybody. They seek identity, as Monica Manheimer describes, but they do not seek freedom or liberation. These concepts have very little meaning for me. We are not free from our past, we are never free of the claims of others, and we ought to not wish to be. (Existential thought, and emphasis on the *acte gratuite*, has always seemed to me a very inadequate way of looking at life.) We are all part of a long inheritance, a human community in which we must play our proper part.[54]

People, Drabble believes, have very little free will; all human activities are planned. In another telling quote Drabble explains these views: "accidents are all planned, and one's fate is planned. It is going to contain certain accidents. There's nothing you can do about it. I was teaching *Oedipus* last week and, indeed, the idea that whatever you do is all written up for you and that the accidents are simply part of some bigger plan made up at some other date by somebody else is fascinating."[55] Furthermore, Drabble feels that because there is an ultimate reason for everything that happens, one should not fight one's fate. She expounds her belief by means of an example: "There's a very strong element of [fatalism] in me because I really wish to believe that God has ordered the world correctly and that if he ordered you to be a depressive, then he meant something very significant by it and that if you be depressive, then God will illumine you in the end. Whereas if you try and cheat God by taking pills or doing this, that, or the other, then you won't get what God planned for you, which is something very special."[56]

Although many of the critics have discussed the role of fate in Drabble's novels, no one has done a full-scale analysis of her particular philosophy of fatalism. Since the central concern of her fiction is human beings' lack of free will, such an extensive investigation is called for. It is the purpose of this study to examine the various forces that Drabble sees as shaping and determining human beings' lives. These include a metaphysical force, or fate; nature; and the family. All of these forces operate to keep a person from being able to act completely freely and rationally. Furthermore, they contribute to the formation of identity: one is not free to become what one will, as existentialists hold, for there are aspects of identity that are nonrational and atavistic. Drabble emphasizes these aspects, showing that a human being is a cog in the universe, an instrument of nature, and a link in a family chain.

Drabble's heavy determinism makes for a rather harsh view of life. And yet what emerges from her fiction is a feeling of hope. For she suggests, as some of the critics have noted, that in submitting to the controlling forces and bonds of life one achieves wisdom, strength, and a profound understanding of what it means to be a human being. Such submission results in a state of grace. She explains, "being in harmony with some other purpose is a state of grace. When you're not fighting it, it might simply be being in tune with your fate, like Oedipus. It is then that you're in a state of grace. Once you set yourself up against it in the wrong way, you're out of grace."[57] Furthermore, although their actions and identities are largely determined, human beings can achieve freedom through their imaginations. Drabble's protagonists often live bleak lives, but their imaginations are rich and productive.

Drabble's concerns, then, go beyond the condition of contemporary women. Even in her early novels she implies these wider concerns, although she presents them in the forms they assume in the lives of young women. But a retrospective examination of these novels, from the vantage point of her most recent ones, reveals that the concerns were there from the beginning. Although she is interested in the particular problems of contemporary existence and renders them with convincing realism, she is always looking behind them at the universal, timeless issues of which they are a manifestation. And her response to these issues is at odds with contemporary attitudes, for she upholds a set of values and a philosophical view that hark back to preexistential times. Human beings are not free, she declares; they are embedded in structures and subject to forces over which their rational selves have little control: a universe ruled by an omnipotent deity; nature; and the family. If they try to struggle against these forces they will be miserable; if they submit to them they will find grace and solace. And finally, human beings have their imaginations, which enable them to endure existence by imbuing it with richness and significance.

2

Drabble's Dark Universe

Margaret Drabble's novels portray a bleak, often menacing universe, governed by a harsh supernatural force that allows human beings very little free will. This curiously old-fashioned view apears in a fictional world which is otherwise contemporary. Most of her protagonists reflect this paradox: they are intellectual, often cynical people living in a society of existential choices and situational ethics, and yet they use concepts such as providence, sin, and grace in contemplating their lives. In this respect the characters resemble their author. She too lives a sophisticated, contemporary outer life while guided by an inner life replete with Bunyanesque notions, symbols, and fears.[1] While unsure of her exact theological stance and beliefs, she continues to be influenced by the religious teachings in her background.[2] She grew up in the Yorkshire area, where Methodism, with its emphasis on "bleeding wounds and fountains of blood and loads of sin," had prevailed since the eighteenth century.[3] Although her mother eventually rejected religion and became an atheist, Drabble as a child was heavily exposed to her maternal grandparents' hellfire-and-brimstone beliefs.[4] She was also, as Valerie Myer demonstrates, influenced by the pervasive puritan climate that has lingered on in the more provincial regions of England. She was infected not only by puritanism's secular attitudes—hard work, frugality, a strong sense of personal responsibility—but also by its belief in fate and predestination.

The general influences of puritanism and Methodism are revealed in a number of ways in Drabble's fiction, ranging from the fatalistic universe she portrays to her characters' habits of spiritual introspection and ruminating on Biblical stories.[5] Of course, the question of exact causes is always a difficult one to answer, and Drabble's metaphysic is probably not entirely the result of these religious influences. They are doubtless significant, but they may be effects rather than causes. That is, it may be that Drabble's innate temperament, her deep-seated need to perceive a divine plan at work in the universe, attracts her to any religion that answers this need.[6] In *The Ice Age*, for example, she implies an attraction to the medieval Christian views of Boethius. And in her interview with Nancy Hardin she revealed an affinity with the fatalistic religion of pagan Greece: "I'm kind of Greek with a Greek view of the gods, I think. I mean, better keep on the right side of them because although they're not very nice, they're exceedingly powerful. One had better appreciate it."[7]

Drabble's fatalistic world view has literary as well as religious antecedents. Her outlook bears some striking similarities to Thomas Hardy's. Both novelists emphasize the way fate usually works against the individual's earthly happiness, a situation which causes them to suspect the existence of a malicious deity who delights in thwarting and playing tricks on human beings. Drabble, like Hardy, is highly sensitive to the cruel ironies and accidents of life that would seem to imply such a deity, and her works are filled with such incidents. In fact, John Updike has accused her of being "shamelessly dependent upon coincidence."[8] However, for Drabble this reliance is not a handy plot device but a reflection of her belief in a divine meaning behind all accidents.[9] The attitude expressed by Rosamund Stacey, the protagonist of *The Millstone*, undoubtedly reflects Drabble's own: "I thought for some time about life's little ironies, for the truth was . . . that they always moved me out of all proportion to their significance in any respectable philosophic scheme. I have always been stirred, sometimes profoundly, by newspaper comments such as Killed While Adjusting Safety Belt, or Collapsed Night Before Wedding" (*Millstone*, p. 74). Because Rosamund is ordinarily a rational person, she is perplexed by her occasional gravitation toward "some absurd belief in a malicious deity" (*Millstone*, p. 74), a belief which causes her to fear that misfortune may descend upon her at any moment. For this reason she will never "tempt fate" (*Millstone*, p. 158) by making plans or harboring hopes that could be knocked down by the whim of such a deity.

Many Drabble protagonists display similar superstitious leanings. They frequently ponder whether random events are true accidents or the result of a divine plan. Emma Evans of *The Garrick Year*, for instance, reads with fascination a newspaper article on survivors of a disastrous airplane crash over the ocean because "it is interesting, to know what people think who unexpectedly survive death, whether it seems to them to be coincidence or providence" (*Garrick Year*, p. 124). She believes that "there's a providence in the fall of a sparrow" (*Garrick Year*, p. 112). Several characters in *The Ice Age* wonder why life is filled with so many undeserved evils and misfortunes— whether these are a divine "joke, a trial, [or] a punishment" (*Ice Age*, p. 182). Jane Gray of *The Waterfall*, perhaps because she is the most passive of all the protagonists, is the most firmly convinced that all accidents and ills are the result of a divine plan. She believes that there is "something sacred in her fate that she [dares] not countermand by effort" (*Waterfall*, pp. 3–4) and that "providence [can] deal with her without her own assistance" (*Waterfall*, p. 4). However, she is acutely aware that this divine plan is usually at odds with human desires and well-being and that we live in a "hostile, ill-ordered universe" (*Waterfall*, p. 182). And so Jane reflects, "Perhaps I could take a religion that denied free will, that placed God in his true place, arbitrary, carelessly kind, idly malicious, intermittently attentive, and himself subject, as Zeus was, to necessity" (*Waterfall*, p. 56).

Drabble herself is subject to the same sense of doom that haunts many of her characters. She has described feeling "all the time that the axe is about to fall and whenever I'm particularly happy, I'm more than ever afraid."[10] This sense of imminent disaster, the feeling that happiness and security are fragile, ephemeral conditions, runs through all Drabble's books—even her relatively sunny novels such as *The Realms of Gold*—and finds its ultimate expression in the doomsday vision of *The Ice Age*.

A major way Drabble creates an ominous atmosphere is by showing the importance of the newspaper in her characters' lives. In her early novels, where the protagonists are absorbed in their own personal experiences and private worlds, the newspaper serves as a connection with external reality, and this reality is filled with disasters, accidents, and injustices. Rosamund Stacey's fascination with newspaper articles demonstrating life's cruel ironies has already been mentioned. Emma Evans and Janet Bird, housebound young mothers, hungrily read newspapers in their spare moments, and are struck by the prevalence of disaster in the world. Alison Murray is also drawn to disaster stories: horrified but compelled, she reads a gruesome account in *The Times* of a woman being blown to pieces by a bomb. Kitty Friedmann (*Ice Age*) is moved to tears by newspaper stories on human suffering. In the *Evening Standard* she reads an article "about a baby who was suffering from a rare bone disease: his mother was appealing for a donor, for new bone marrow. Kitty Friedmann's eyes filled with tears. Poor little lad. Poor woman. Beneath the article about the baby was a brief report of an old man who had been kicked to death and robbed of forty pence on Wimbledon Common. She read this too. She continued to cry" (*Ice Age*, p. 58). Although Kitty has "always had the greatest difficulty in believing in the existence of ill luck," occasionally "faint shadows of doubt reached her: how, in this day and age, could a child die, slowly, publicly, foredoomed, of an incurable disease, how could an old man be kicked to death?" (*Ice Age*, pp. 58–59). Frances Wingate is similarly moved to tears by a story in *The Times* about a baby whose father battered it to death.

The newspaper figures heavily in Drabble's novels undoubtedly because the author regards it as a particularly powerful reminder of life's evils and the randomness of fate. She has claimed to be "so susceptible to horror that reading the newspaper is enough for [her]: when [she] actually see[s] the news on television it makes [her] feel terrible for days."[11] Simon Camish of *The Needle's Eye* holds a similar attitude:

> On Saturday morning, Simon decided that he would do some gardening. He had depressed himself so thoroughly by reading the newspapers that he felt he had to do something. The newspapers, for a holiday weekend, had been full of unimaginable disasters. An earthquake in the Middle East had killed tens of thousands, and cholera was breaking out amidst the survivors: There was an account of a trial in the States over an alleged massacre in Vietnam. Three men in an iron works in Yorkshire had been killed by molten slag from a mobile ladle. A child in a mental home had fallen into a bath of scalding water and had died five days later of burns. There had been a twenty-car pile-up on the M1. Mr. Calvacoressi said that it would cost his wife a fortune to reclaim her baby. So Simon dug his garden. (*Needle's Eye*, p. 270)

In addition to using newspaper headlines and articles, Drabble also draws attention to life's evils by presenting a gallery of miserable human predicaments. The ill, the poor, and the downtrodden appear in her books and illustrate how painful life is for vast numbers of human beings. The unfairness and horror of their conditions is underscored by the fact that most of them are highly undeserving of their cruel fates. Many are innocent children: the autistic youngsters that Sarah Bennett views in a television documentary; the small working-class child in *The Millstone* who receives a taste of life's bitter unfairness at an early age when she is deprived of playmates because the fastidious middle-class parents in the neighborhood will not allow their children to associate with her; Rosamund Stacey's infant daughter, who suddenly develops a mysterious, pernicious heart disease that will shadow her for life; the severely retarded child of the protagonist in Drabble's short story "Crossing the Alps" (1971);[12] Alison Murray's daughter Molly, mentally and physically crippled since birth with cerebral palsy. The misfortune of Kitty Friedmann—random IRA terrorism has killed her husband and crippled her—also seems highly undeserved, for she is an exceptionally good woman, who has never harmed anyone in her life. And it is particularly cruel that Alison Murray's sister Rosemary, who has always lived in the shadow of Alison's beauty, should become disfigured by breast cancer while Alison maintains her lovely figure into middle age.

Drabble gives an affecting portrait of those bowed down by poverty and illness in *The Millstone*. Rosamund, having grown up in an upper-middle-class environment, has been sheltered from the spectacle of poverty until her pregnancy, when she begins attending a National Health clinic in a working-class neighborhood. Here she is "reduced almost to tears by the variety of human misery that presented itself" (*Millstone*, p. 64). She witnesses anemic, exhausted women, worn out by numerous pregnancies and children and by the endless effort of trying to make ends meet, reduced to an attitude of passive, stoical endurance. Rosamund is deeply disturbed by this exposure to "facts of inequality, of limitation, of separation, of the impossible, heartbreaking uneven hardship of the human lot" (*Millstone*, p. 77). It convinces her that life is not fair: "It is unfair on every score and every count and in every particular, and those, who, like my [Fabian Socialist] parents, attempt to level it out are doomed to failure" (*Millstone*, pp. 93–94).

Rosamund's acute awareness of life's basic unfairness is shared by many of the protagonists and by Drabble herself, who has said, "Equality and egalitarianism preoccupy me constantly, and not very hopefully."[13] Sarah Bennett is obsessed by the blatantly unequal distribution of life's goods. She senses that there is something very wrong with a world in which she has been given so many physical and intellectual gifts while her dowdy cousin Daphne's share is so meager. And she is appalled by the fact that "some people are born to a smooth life" (*Bird-Cage*, p. 96), like her happily married friend Stephanie, whereas others, like her poor friend Gill, whose husband has left her, are destined for a rocky, tearful course. Although Sarah tries to justify these discrepancies by reminding herself of the "Greater gifts—greater duties to society" maxim, this answer strikes her as inadequate. Her query, "Why do you think God made people like Daphne?" (*Bird-Cage*, p. 180), is a variation of the same basic question that haunts many of Drabble's characters and runs through all her books. Karel Schmidt of *The Realms of Gold* puts it this way: "There was no justice in life, why seek for it or try to create it? What justice could ever have given to him and Frances such years of loving, and to others, no loving at all?" (*Realms*, p. 217). Again and again Drabble's characters come up against the hard fact that life's fortunes and misfortunes are unevenly doled out.

Besides the unequal distribution of human happiness, another cruel condition of life that preoccupies Drabble is the inevitable disappointment of youthful dreams in the face of adult realities. Her analysis of Wordsworth's "Imortality Ode" reveals a great deal about her own attitude. Whereas most readers find in Wordsworth's poem an argument that the philosophical joys of adulthood are compensation for the loss of the intense, spontaneous joys of childhood, Drabble finds, on the contrary, an attitude of acute loss: "It is essentially a middle-aged poem, and for Wordsworth it is something of a swan song. He does his best to close it on a note of optimism and hope, but nevertheless what comes across most powerfully from the poem is a feeling of anguished regret for what is lost. However nobly he resolves to bear his loss, resolution itself can never make up for what is gone, and he knows it."[14]

The label "middle-aged" may equally well be applied to Drabble's own vision, for in many of her works she focuses on the compromises and disappointments of adulthood, especially resignation to the fact that one's youthful dreams will never be realized. Although in her later novels she presents certain middle-aged characters who have learned to be content with "life's modest satisfactions" (*Needle's Eye*, p. 219), the protagonists of her earlier works and some of the younger characters in her later works are acutely distressed by the deflation of these dreams.

The experience of coming to terms with the bleak realities of adult life is the focus of Drabble's first novel, *A Summer Bird-Cage*. The action, which takes place during the year after the protagonist graduates from Oxford, consists of a series of experiences that open her eyes to the discrepancy between her undergraduate dreams and the real world. While at the university Sarah had envisioned a life of moral and aesthetic beauty, friendship, love, and equality, but the life she encounters as a working girl living in a London bedsitter is a far cry from this. Her friendships, in college so lofty and generous, now easily become threatened by petty bickering, for she and her friends find it hard to remain above meanness and irritability when they have to worry about money and scraping along. She is also dismayed by the education she receives about marriage. At Oxford she carried on a sublime, idealistic love affair and is still involved in it long-distance while her boyfriend is spending the year on a fellowship at Harvard. However, her ideals regarding marriage are dealt a severe blow by her exposure to the inadequate marriages of various friends and relatives, many of which deteriorate because of lack of money, a sudden pregnancy, or misunderstanding about roles. But, most important, she discovers that life after college is inevitably a downhill course for women of her generation. Although the novel's action takes place in the early 1960s, women think in terms of either a career or marriage, not both. Yet Sarah, intensely alive both intellectually and emotionally, wants both: "I should like to bear leaves and flowers and fruit, I should like the whole world" (Bird-Cage, p. 77). She explains to someone who asks her why she has not embarked on an academic career, "You can't be a sexy don" (Bird-Cage, p. 198). She therefore postpones making a commitment to either marriage or a career for as long as possible, for she knows that as soon as she chooses one she will have to relinquish her dreams of the other.

In other novels Drabble offers portraits of young women who have in fact made the choice of marriage and suffer bitterly from the ensuing constriction of their horizons. Emma Evans, a young wife and mother, forced to give up the prospect of an interesting career in London and move to the provinces because of her husband's job, grimly reflects, "I could hardly believe that marriage was going to deprive me of this too. It had already deprived me of so many things which I had childishly overvalued: my independence, my income, my twenty-two inch waist, my sleep, most of my friends . . . and many more indefinite attributes like hope and expectation" (Garrick Year, p. 11).

Janet Bird and Jane Gray have also been sorely let down by marriage and its accompanying restrictions. They have consequently grown indifferent toward life. Emma sums up this feeling of lost possibilities when she muses, "what had happened to me, that I, who had seemed cut out for some extremity or other, should be here now bending over a washing machine to pick out a button or two and some bits of soggy wet cotton? What chances were there now for the once-famous Emma, whose name had been in certain small exclusive circles the cause for so much discussion and prediction?" (*Garrick Year*, p. 139).

Drabble's theme of the disappointment of youthful dreams is particularly poignant when she applies it to working-class characters. In her short story "The Gifts of War" (1970), the protagonist's adult life, which consists of penury, hard work, and a violent marriage, is a grim contrast to the future she had envisioned as an adolescent. With bitter irony the woman recalls the hopes she and her girlhood friends once harbored:

> [she was] penniless then as now, but still hopeful, still endowed with the touching faith that if by some miracle she could buy a pair of nylons or a particular blue lace blouse or a new brand of lipstick, then deliverance would be granted to her in the form of money, marriage, romance, the visiting prince who would glimpse her in the crowd, glorified by that seductive blouse, and carry her off to a better world. She could remember so well how hopeful they had been: even Betty Jones, fat, monstrous, ludicrous Betty Jones had cherished such rosy illusions. . . . Time had taught Betty Jones: she shuffled now in shoes cracked and splitting beneath her weight. Time had taught them all. The visiting prince, whom need and desire had once truly transfigured in her eyes, now lay there at home in bed, stubbly, disgusting, ill, malingering, unkind: she remembered the girl who had seen such other things in him with a contemptuous yet pitying wonder.[15]

Eileen Sharkey, Rose Vassiliou's nineteen-year-old neighbor in *The Needle's Eye*, is another working-class girl with similar notions about escaping her squalid, tedious existence. She dreams of being a "Spanish duchess, or a wicked woman, or a make-up girl at the B.B.C." (*Needle's Eye*, p. 157). Mistakenly assuming, as does the protagonist of "The Gifts of War," that love and marriage will effect the glorious life she desires, she hurls herself into an affair and gets pregnant. But the man won't marry her and she is left facing her dreary life, stuck in it forever, she realizes, now that she is saddled with a baby. Rose, gazing at Eileen's glum, depressed countenance, sadly observes, "There she sat, nineteen, finished, excluded for ever from what she might want to be" (*Needle's Eye*, p. 252). Rose further reflects on what a terrible moment it is when "one abandons possibility. Gone was Eileen the wicked lady, driving around in taxis, wearing fur coats, drinking cocktails: gone was Eileen the make-up girl with false eyelashes and a pink overall: gone was Eileen the garage man's girl, taking trips up the motorway in a fast car" (*Needle's Eye*, p. 253).

Drabble, then, repeatedly emphasizes the powerlessness of human beings against the inimical conditions of life. While this concern appears in all of her fiction, it does not become the central focus of a work until *The Ice Age*. Drabble here makes use of the medieval wheel-of-fortune concept, presenting a wide range of characters who have recently plummetted from fortunate to unfortunate situations. Anthony Keating has suffered a sudden, premature heart attack and lost a great deal of money in the recent property slump. Alison Murray's teenage daughter has been imprisoned and sentenced to hard labor for her part in a fatal accident in a Balkan communist country. Kitty and Max Friedmann were celebrating their Ruby wedding anniversary in a Mayfair restaurant when an IRA bomb exploded, killing Max and maiming Kitty. Len Wincobank, a fallen real-estate tycoon, has been banished to prison for having bribed a town councillor in an effort to redeem a property investment. The particular woes of the individual characters are set against the background of the public woes of contemporary Britain: the collapsing economy, workers' strikes, the Irish troubles, and Britain's shrinking international prestige and power.

As in earlier novels, but here more explicitly, the question of why undeserved evil occurs is raised. The narrator reflects that "it was puzzling that so many dreadful things had happened in so short a space of time. Why Kitty, why Max, why Anthony Keating? And why had the punishments been so unrelated to the offenses?" (*Ice Age*, p. 6). Appalled by the thought that human beings have no control over their own happiness, Alison in a moment of desperation attempts to convince herself of the existence of free will by inventing an ingenious theory to prove that we "make our own ordering" of happiness or sorrow (*Ice Age*, p. 247). The narrator sympathizes with her need but implies that she is deluded: "who can be surprised that one so subject to the blows of circumstance should attempt to see in them a possibility of self-will, freedom, choice?" (*Ice Age*, p. 247).

Of course, ultimately Alison cannot accept her own theory: "Facts belied it. There is no comfort, no sustenance" (*Ice Age*, p. 247). Indeed, so convinced has she become of the existence of a malicious deity that she has grown to expect the worst and is surprised when any happiness does come her way. When she and Anthony are granted an evening of peace and unalloyed happiness, she wonders "what remote sense of fair play in heaven had allowed such remission" (*Ice Age*, p. 247).

This impression of the individual powerless in the face of large menacing powers that rule the universe is created not only by the content of the novel—the disasters and misfortunes that beset the characters—but also by its narrative technique. An omniscient narrator ranges over a wide number of characters from an Olympian height, reporting on their tragedies and misfortunes. Indeed, his view encompasses all of Britain: "A huge icy fist, with large cold fingers," he informs us, "was squeezing and chilling the people of Britain, that great and puissant nation, slowing down their blood, locking them into immobility, fixing them in a solid stasis, like fish in a frozen river" (*Ice Age*, p. 60). This godlike perspective has the effect of dwarfing human beings, emphasizing their relative powerlessness over the course of events.

The Middle Ground also presents an apocalyptic vision, although here it does not occupy center stage. Rather, it forms the backdrop to the story of Kate Armstrong's struggle with the despair of middle age. Whereas in the early novels characters merely read about disasters in the newspaper, here, as in *The Ice Age*, tragedy constantly intrudes upon their own lives. Kate's two best friends are seriously injured in bizarre accidents: Hugo Mainwaring, a foreign correspondent, has had his arm shot off in an international incident in Eritrea; Evelyn Stennett is badly burned and temporarily blinded while trying to settle a violent domestic dispute in her capacity of social worker. In addition, Hugo's young son has become brain-damaged as a result of an accidental overdose of anesthesia administered during a routine operation; the son of Kate's Lebanese friend has been killed in a street battle in Beirut; and Kate herself accidentally conceives a child that prenatal tests reveal to be severely deformed and that Kate, after much mental torture, decides to have aborted.

Drabble piles tragedy upon tragedy in this novel, giving the impression that the world is hurtling toward some kind of ultimate disaster. This is further enhanced by the vision of decadence and violence that daily meets the characters' eyes. London's subways and streets are littered with posters revealing racial hatred. British youth, including Kate's and Evelyn's own children, engage in aimless, often destructive behavior out of a disaffection with traditional values. Characters are constantly struck by images, real and imagined, of modern life's cruelty and indifference: dead birds, cats, and babies; elderly, ragged people wandering the city streets. In sum, the London of *The Middle Ground* is a decadent, depressing spectacle.

Given the dismal nature of Drabble's fictional universe, it is no wonder that many of her characters have difficulty bearing up. In fact, her books contain a large number of people who are psychologically unstable, some of whom eventually commit suicide. Drabble appears fascinated by the psychological response of people so extremely sensitive to life's ills that they cannot function normally. She creates five characters who suffer from this syndrome. In *Jerusalem the Golden* Phillipa Denham finds life so painful that she cries openly in the streets, haunted by an intolerable grief. She claims that "it was injustice that made her weep" (*Jerusalem*, p. 167), explaining to her husband that "she could not bear to have more of anything than anyone in the world and that misery seemed to her to be a duty" (*Jerusalem*, p. 167). And indeed, her emaciated, pallid appearance reveals her masochistic attitude. So incapacitating is her distress that she can barely perform ordinary daily acts like taking care of her children and her home, going to the store, and chatting with her neighbors. Believing that life is a hopeless, miserable affair, she fatalistically submits to her affliction.

Throughout most of *The Waterfall*, Jane Gray is similarly disposed. Her symptoms strongly resemble Phillipa's. The ordinary acts of existence that others perform perfunctorily are for her an immense ordeal. She is amazed that people can "continue to live, as though life were a practical possibility" (*Waterfall*, p. 193), and she wonders "how they all [manage] it, how they [manage] to keep alive, when life [is] so difficult. For herself, she [has] almost given up" (*Waterfall*, pp. 47–48). She can "hardly force herself to walk along a street or ask a grocer for a pound of sprouts" (*Waterfall*, p. 127). Fatalistically acquiescing to her condition, she becomes a near-recluse, doing the minimum to survive and allowing herself and her home to deteriorate physically. As does Phillipa, Jane demonstrates the response of a delicate, sensitive psychological constitution to the spectacle of life's basic injustice and the overwhelming misery of the human lot. She points out, "The principle of natural selection has always haunted me: each day—truly, I am serious, each day—I try to batter out for myself some principle of equality that might apply to the savage and indifferent world. I fail, of course" (*Waterfall*, p. 148).

Beata of *The Realms of Gold* possesses the same psychological make up as Phillipa and Jane. She is only lightly sketched and kept in the background, but her similarity to the other women is marked. She too is neurotic, reticent, and so fatally passive that she does not properly take care of herself. She eventually develops anorexia nervosa and has to be spoon-fed throughout her pregnancy. After her baby is born, she turns her back to the world and takes to her bed, where she remains for the rest of the novel, inert and indifferent. The root cause of her lassitude is similar to Phillipa's and Jane's: she believes that "the conditions of survival [are] so dreadful that it [is] undignified to survive" and that "living is a crime" (*Realms*, p. 88).

Beata's husband, Stephen Ollerenshaw, suffers from the same sensibility. He is abnormally conscious of the physical horrors that afflict mankind. Although young, in good health, and from a materially well-off background, he is obsessed with mortality and decay:

> Being alive was sordid, degrading, sickly, unimaginable: to struggle on through another fifty years, tormented by fear and guilt and sorrow, was a fate nobody should ever embrace. . . . Man had been created sick and dying: for seventy years he feebly struggled to avoid his proper end. There was something overwhelmingly disgusting about man's efforts, against all odds, to stay alive. One spent one's life in inoculating oneself, swallowing medicaments, trying to destroy disease, and all to no end, for the end was death. (*Realms*, p. 344)

Concluding that it is better to be dead than alive, he takes his own life and that of his infant daughter, for he cannot bear the thought of her growing up and facing the horrid conditions of existence.

Finally, Susan Sondersheim, who makes a brief but memorable appearance in *The Middle Ground*, is another such psychologically fragile creature. Attending a dinner party at the home of Kate's friends the Stennetts, she casts a gloom upon what would otherwise have been a jolly occasion. Like Phillipa, Jane, and Beata, she is excessively thin and indifferent to food and apparently unable to take any pleasure or comfort from life. She behaves in an inappropriate, distracted manner, her only contribution to the conversation being an odd, seemingly pointless anecdote about coming upon a dead cat, which she at first took to be a dead baby, while walking the beach in Sierra Leone. To the bafflement of the rest of the company, she then leaves the table and locks herself into the bathroom, where she remains, audibly moaning and crying, for the rest of the dinner. Although the specific cause of her mental imbalance is kept obscure, her manner implies an acute uncomfortableness with life.

These five characters, then, owing to peculiarly sensitive psychological constitutions, battle with despair. There are in addition to this particular form many other instances of mental illness scattered throughout Drabble's fiction. In *The Middle Ground* Hugo's wife Judith becomes maniacally obsessed with revenge after the accident that brain-damaged their son. Kate's brother has suffered a nervous breakdown and has become unbalanced by his jealousy of Kate, and Kate's mother is an agoraphobic, her father a paranoid. In *The Ice Age* Alison Murray, distraught by her personal difficulties and the immense public problems of her nation, suffers a temporary nervous breakdown. In *The Realms of Gold* in addition to Stephen's suicide, there is reference to the suicide of Frances' older sister, Alice, and to the madness of various relatives and ancestors. Julian of *The Garrick Year* commits suicide, and Jane Gray of *The Waterfall* mentions having "great-uncles in asylums up and down the country, and [her] father's father killed himself" (*Waterfall*, p. 136). The protagonist of "Crossing the Alps" once tried to take her own life and that of her retarded child. In *Jerusalem the Golden* the eldest Denham daughter is mad, and while Clara is visiting Paris she is disturbed by the spectacle of a madwoman who wanders the city streets mumbling to herself. Finally, in *A Summer Bird-Cage* there is mention of a television program about schizophrenic children who completely cut themselves off from the real world and construct private little worlds of their own. Sarah, recalling the program, reflects, "The psychiatrist kept insisting that the condition was rare and biochemical, but it seemed oddly metaphysical to me" (*Bird-Cage*, p. 165).

Drabble's view of mental illness would seem to coincide with Sarah's: it is a reasonable, or at least understandable, response to a harsh universe, and not simply a disease. Although her protagonists all ultimately prove to be resilient and able to survive life's torments, they are not unaffected by the dismal perceptions that obsess her mentally ill characters. Indeed, the protagonists must struggle to align themselves with the forces of light and life and sanity, for the forces of darkness and death and insanity loom large in Drabble's universe. Simon Camish, for example, must wrestle with these demons, which occasionally plunge him into despair. At such times he thinks,

there was no light, or none that man might enter: he could
create for himself an ordered darkness, an equality of misery,
a justice in the sharing of the darkness, his own hole, by right,
in that darkness, and his sense of light, his illuminations, were
an evolutionary freak, an artificial glow that had etiolated him
into hopeless pale unnatural underground yellow green de-
formities, a light misreflected through some unintended
chink, too far away for such low creatures ever to reach it and
flourish by it. He might as well lose his eyes, man. He might as
well grow blind, like a fish in his white plated armoury. (*Needle's Eye*, p. 172)

Reflections on human insignificance in a universe largely inimical,
or at best indifferent, also haunt Frances occasionally. At these
times, when "all culture, all process, all human effort" (*Realms*, p.
347) strike her as futile, she finds herself posing the same question
her despondent nephew Stephen has put to her: how can one
possibly imagine that the things one does are worth doing? Stephen
and others regard Frances as a super-woman—robust, strong,
hopeful—and there is much truth behind this appearance; but it is
with an effort that she maintains this attitude. Like the other protagonists, she must force herself to push on against life's pains and
injustices. She frequently turns to alcohol to help her endure periods
of despair. And at particularly bad times she has even "thought she
would like to live her life under an anesthetic. She wasn't up to it; she
would fail, yet again." She reflects, "Too much of the world was
inhospitable, intractable" (*Realms*, p. 54).

Kate Armstrong is another protagonist whose natural robustness
sometimes falters in the face of life's horrors. To maintain sanity
requires a conscious effort when mental illness and violence are
rampant, and Kate is all too aware of how easy it would be to lose
one's footing: "Sanity and madness. Well, certainly, sanity is a precarious state, a thin ridge, a tightrope. However do most of us keep
upright? Like tightrope walkers, by not looking to either side, I
suppose, like horses in blinkers. I should never have looked. I should
never have looked, I should never have looked" (*Middle Ground*, p.
134).

This, then, is the universe of Margaret Drabble, a bleak, dreary,
often menacing place, in which an apparent indifference to human
happiness invites superstitious speculations about a malicious deity.
Given these conditions, she implies, the vast amount of psychological

disease in the world is understandable. Yet ultimately, after portraying these miseries, Drabble affirms life and asserts the possibility of survival in this world. Although her vision is similar to Thomas Hardy's, it is not nearly as dark: her protagonists are not finally tragic figures, as his are. In spite of the disasters and disappointments that come their way, none of the protagonists do themselves in, as do Sue Bridehead and Father Time, or are done in by life, as are Tess of the D'Urbervilles and Jude Fawley. This is because Drabble, "a great believer in surviving," advocates enduring life's difficulties and pushing on.[16] Her protagonists, like herself, "go on relentlessly to the end, trying to make sense of [life], trying to endure it or survive it or see something in it."[17] She explains: "I admire endurance and I admire the courage to come back. . . . I know people who have gone through unbelievable torments and have still got up in the morning and got their children to school . . . . People often ask me why my characters don't just give up and plunge into the depths and be better for it. Yes, but they can't."[18]

However, endurance in Drabble's world does not mean simply stoical resignation to life's bleakness—although a certain amount of this is involved. Rather, Drabble believes that in spite of the darkness that surrounds human existence, individuals experience occasional moments of profound peace and joy. These are gratuitous, ephemeral moments, but they are a source of spiritual nourishment for her protagonists. These experiences do not take place on a grand scale; on the contrary, they usually occur in ordinary, low-key, often domestic situations. But in these moments the protagonists are flooded with a sudden acute awareness and appreciation of the beauty inherent in ordinary, limited human existence, a beauty which they customarily do not perceive. These experiences appear in all Drabble's novels but especially in her last four. In these the protagonists are older and have learned to appreciate more fully such rare good moments, realizing that happiness is not going to come to them on a grand scale, as they had hoped in their youths. Rose and Simon experience such a moment in "the simple pleasure of walking together" (*Needle's Eye*, p. 299), and Rose derives profound joy from "such ordinary signals in the world. Cut prices and sunshine and babies in prams and talking in the shops" (*Needle's Eye*, p. 99). Frances has one of these moments when she and her lover, Karel, stop for lunch at a roadside restaurant:

> "I enjoyed deciding to buy this sandwich," said Karel. "And now I'm going to enjoy eating it."

And hearing him speak, she shivered slightly, as though a moment of intense joy had come to its proper completion, and it occurred to her that she had never been as happy in her life as she was there, sitting at that shabby table gazing through a white net curtain at the road, with two half-eaten sandwiches in front of her, signifying union. To have it was one thing: to know one was having it was something else, more than one could ever have hoped for.

Of such things did life consist. She enjoyed it all. (*Realms*, p. 66)

In *The Middle Ground* these blissful moments often occur when a group of family members or close friends are gathered together eating, drinking, and talking. Suddenly one or more of the characters are flooded with happiness and a profound appreciation of the ordinary human comforts they are partaking of. Coupled with the feeling is a sense of temporary safety, of keeping life's menaces at bay for awhile. Drabble effects this atmosphere by including a threatening element of some sort in the situation. At the Stennetts' dinner party, for example, this element takes the form of Susan Sondersheim, whose odd, sad behavior serves as a reminder of how easy it is to be undone by life. As soon as she and her husband depart the party, the uneasy atmosphere is replaced by a buoyant joyfulness: Ted and Kate "sat down again at the table, helping themselves hungrily to more cheese, to great slices of brown bread, pouring themselves more wine, urging Hugo to more wine. They ate and drank, the survivors, excited, exhilirated, their lease on life renewed by the precarious tenure of others" (*Middle Ground*, p. 48). Their tight circle of joviality temporarily wards off the demons of despair that often haunt the three of them.

Ten years before this episode, Evelyn, Kate, Hugo, and Judith had gathered with their several small children around the Stennett kitchen table one dark December afternoon, eating tea and toast. Although it was an ordinary, low-key occasion, Hugo remembers it as an oasis of happy tranquillity in the midst of the troubles that were besieging them all at the time—money worries, children's illnesses, their own or their spouses' infidelities. For a moment they were happy simply to be enjoying the easy companionship of good friends, the joy of holding their little ones on their laps, and the comfort of a hot cup of tea on a cold afternoon. Hugo recalls the charmed circle they formed: "Evelyn got up and drew the blinds. It was very pleasant in her warm bright kitchen all those years ago, the darkness shut out, the children safely assembled" (*Middle Ground*, p. 167).

Besides such intermittent moments of happiness, humor keeps Drabble's fictional world from becoming finally tragic. In spite of their bleak outlooks, the protagonists are capable of laughing at themselves and their situations.[19] Furthermore, Drabble creates occasional comic scenes that deflate potential tragedy: characters who have been taking themselves or their problems very seriously will suddenly revert to an ordinary, mundane concern, and the change creates an anti-climax. The effect of this kind of humor is to make the ordinary and human appear delightful and lovable.

This comic pattern first appears in the final scene of *A Summer Bird-Cage*. Louise, the protagonist's older sister, has maintained the reputation of a glamorous, distant person, conducting her life on an elevated, dramatic level. Sarah's difficult relationship with her underscores the former's sense of alienation and loneliness, which has been the subject of the novel. However, toward the end of the narrative, Louise suddenly reveals to her sister a very human, vulnerable side of herself. Sarah recounts Louise's description of having been caught by her husband in the bathtub with her lover: "when Stephen went and caught them together in the bath, what upset her most was that she was wearing her bathcap. To keep her hair dry. She said she would have started a scene if she had had her hair loose, but with a plastic hat on like that she felt so ridiculous that she couldn't." Sarah concludes, "She must at heart be quite fond of both John [her lover] and me: of John, to have worn it, and of me, to have told it" (*Bird-Cage*, p. 224).

Drabble's comments about her comic impulse, exemplified by this scene, are revealing:

> I think what I'm most surprised about is the fact that [my books are] quite readable and I think, quite amusing. Other people don't agree, but I think they're quite funny. Now this is something that I would never have expected of myself, because I was very keen on tragedy. But when I wrote my first novel and decided that it was going to have a funny ending (the beautiful older sister caught by her husband in the bathtub with her lover) I thought "I'm really going to be a different kind of person!" This is wonderful, I felt. Life is going to be good, not bad.[20]

The novels reflect Drabble's dual tendencies toward tragedy and comedy. The tragic vision is always threatening to take over but is warded off by comic moments. Jane Gray echoes Drabble when she remarks at the end of her narrative, which has told the story of her sublime, perilous love affair with her cousin's husband, "it's hardly a tragic ending, to so potentially a tragic tale. In fact, I am rather ashamed of the amount of amusement that my present life affords me, and of how much I seem to have gained by it" (*Waterfall*, pp. 281–82). Later she observes that her situation has "resolved into comedy, not tragedy" (*Waterfall*, p. 283). Earlier, in the midst of her love affair, Jane had imagined a tragic ending: "Perhaps I'll go mad with guilt, like Sue Bridehead, or drown myself in an effort to reclaim lost renunciations, like Maggie Tulliver" (*Waterfall*, p. 184). But ultimately her sense of humor and her strong practical streak save her. The latter, though largely suppressed during the height of her affair, occasionally emerges, providing a comic contrast to her usual romantic perspective. For example, when she and her lover have just embarked on their secret vacation and are full of amorous talk, the romantic atmosphere is suddenly undercut by the intrusion of a practical, mundane concern: " 'Oh heavens,' she said, in a voice like any woman anywhere, in a voice so like a real voice that it surprised her, 'Oh heavens, I forgot to cancel the papers and the milk' " (*Waterfall*, p. 221).

Drabble uses this deflationary technique to lighten temporarily the seriousness of her characters and help them put life into a more cheerful and balanced perspective. Another example occurs in *The Ice Age*: while traveling in a foreign country, Anthony Keating, in the midst of profound metaphysical speculations which have led him to the revelation that man cannot do without God, suddenly worries that he may have misplaced his passport. "A man without God and without his papers would be truly lost, thought Anthony" (*Ice Age*, p. 265)—a remark which makes fun of his previous train of thought.

In a similar example in *The Middle Ground*, Evelyn Stennett, lying in her hospital bed contemplating Emily Dickinson's and Meister Eckhart's statements on the importance and difficulty of maintaining faith, is suddenly interrupted by the simultaneous arrival of her dinner and her husband. She immediately switches from her disturbing philosophical line of thought to a humorous, practical one, mentally constructing a pun out of the word "infidel" when she spots her husband and is reminded of his marital infidelities, and becoming interested in the dinner menu. Her absorption in practical affairs causes her philosophical concerns to pale in importance: she welcomes Ted's "interesting news that he had found the long-lost radiator bleed key in the bathroom cabinet, information certainly more cheering than any she was likely to find in Emily Dickinson. As for Meister Eckhart, he could wait. She didn't need him yet" (*Middle Ground*, pp. 250–51).

Scenes such as these bring to the forefront Drabble's warring impulses toward the tragic and the comic, toward the serious and the lighthearted. It is as though the author becomes impatient when the former begin to take over and chides herself, "It's all well and good to worry about one's soul and one's place in the universe, but after all there are practical matters to attend to." This ability to assert the importance of the practical and to laugh at one's metaphysical worries is a strategy for survival Drabble shares with all her protagonists.

Thus, in spite of the fact that a human being is a tiny, powerless speck in a turbulent, menacing universe, there are redeeming qualities to the position. There is both beauty and humor in the condition of being human. Drabble's novels hold up for our admiration people who perceive these qualities of life in spite of its prevailing gloom. Although she has deep sympathy for those like Eileen Sharkey who become permanently disillusioned with life, she clearly prefers people like Rose Vassiliou and her friend Emily Offenbach. These two women have, like Eileen, discovered adulthood to be a disappointment after their girlish hopes; however, they do not lose their taste for joy and humor:

> "Christ," they would say to each other, clutching small wailing babies, stewing scrag end, wandering dully round the park. "Christ, if only we'd *known* what we had to *go* through, if only we'd known—" but in the very saying of it, betrayed (in Emily's case) bruised (in Rose's case) and impoverished (in both cases) they had smiled at each other, and laughed, and had experienced happiness. Life had been so much better, and so much worse, than they had expected: what they had not expected was that they were both happy people, incapable of resisting, incapable of failing to discover the gleams of joy. . . . Such things must not be spoken of, they must not be admitted. But why are we alive, at all? (*Needle's Eye*, pp. 222–23)

3

Nature and the Individual

Nature is another force, along with fate, that plays a major role in Drabble's fictional world. Drabble uses the term in a broad, multifarious sense: it encompasses people's innate characters, human and animal biological processes, the natural physical world, and what can only be called "the gifts of nature"—those primordially and universally recognized bounties, such as health, wealth, beauty, and talent, which are dispensed to certain fortunate people. Disparate as these four phenomena are on the surface, they are all manifestations of what Drabble honors as the natural: an inexorable, awesome force, beyond human control, that rolls through all of the animate and inanimate world.

Drabble's concept of nature appears to derive from a mixture of Christian, romantic, and Classical notions. When she talks about the uniqueness and sacredness of each human being, she implies the Christian belief that every person contains a spark of God. Her statement to Nancy Hardin about God's having a special plan for each individual has already been mentioned. But her views on biological nature and the physical world are closer to the romantic than the Christian tradition. Like the Romantics, especially Wordsworth, she wants to reestablish human beings' intimate connection with the rest of nature—animal, vegetative, and geological. And like them, she intuits the presence of a supreme force, be it God or something more abstract, animating and giving significance to the natural world. Although this supernatural force pervades all the world, it seems closer to the surface, or more accessible, in primitive landscapes. As Drabble has observed, "For many of us today, lacking [traditional religious] convictions, the perception of God in nature is as close as we get to religious experience."[1] Finally, Drabble's views on the gifts of nature suggest a Classical sensibility; in particular, her feeling for the ephemerality of such gifts and her belief that one should make the most of them while they last is reminiscent of the Classical *carpe diem* attitude.

In all its four forms, Drabble feels, nature should be respected and submitted to. One should strive to discover and live according to one's own nature, appreciate one's biological processes and drives, recognize one's place in the natural physical world, and cultivate one's natural gifts. For Drabble, conducting one's life in this manner results in spiritual health, or what she calls a state of grace, as well as in a sounder sense of identity. The following sections will examine Drabble's fictional treatment of each of the four aspects of nature.

I

At the end of *The Needle's Eye*, Rose Vassiliou is at Alexandra Palace, gazing at a gritty concrete statue of a lion. She muses appreciatively, "Mass-produced it had been, but it had weathered into identity. And this, she hoped, for every human soul" (*Needle's Eye*, p. 369). These sentiments can be taken to be the author's own, for Drabble believes that each individual is born with an innate nature which, if unimpeded, will surface and flourish in the course of his or her life. She often compares the individual with a plant: if cultivated and given room to grow, the personality will bloom and bear fruit. To develop and live in harmony with one's nature, then, is to live a spiritually and psychologically salubrious life. Drabble has explained, "We can choose to go against our nature, but only very slightly. You can't completely alter what you were given without doing yourself a great violence which means that you go mad or become an ineffective person."[2]

Most of the protagonists share their author's belief. They are constantly invoking their natures to guide or justify their behavior. Even eccentric and self-destructive tendencies are respected. For instance, Emma Evans says of her addiction to expensive, impractical Victorian furnishings and knickknacks, "I know that my attachment to such things, and the importance they assume for me, verge in the eyes of others on the irresponsible. I am not happy that the opinion of such people should be bad, but I am made how I am made" (*Garrick Year*, p. 38). Rose Vassiliou weeps over "the complete and hopeless irredeemability of her own nature" (*Needle's Eye*, p. 47), which causes her to be too weak and trusting with people. Nonetheless, she accepts its inevitability: "she was settled now, and her nature, though it saddened her at times as it had done this evening, she had on the whole so accepted and understood that she felt she could look at its vagaries quite equably, she could watch it panicking over the choice between taxis and buses with something like a maternal amusement. She was what she was: she had learned to go along with it" (*Needle's Eye*, p. 50). Similarly, Kate Armstrong "knows herself trapped by her own good nature and all its defects" and "watches its thrashing and struggling with an amazed and sad detachment" (*Middle Ground*, p. 86).

It is just such a view on the part of Janet Bird that makes her realize there is no way to improve her unhappy, incompatible marriage, for neither her own nor her husband's natures can be changed. And she believes it is important to follow one's nature. For that reason she does not regard as tragic her great-aunt Con's final days, spent in an eccentric, shabby manner in her decaying cottage. She explains her attitude to her cousin Frances: "I feel I am myself, and that I've got to look after it. But I don't know what it is. I know it's there, that's all. That's why I don't think it was at all awful about Aunt Con, she was being herself, if you know what I mean" (*Realms*, p. 320). Frances agrees, and ultimately comes to regard her young nephew Stephen's suicide in the same light: "With a certain admirable determination, he had faced his own nature, and the terms of life and death, and seen what to do" (*Realms*, p. 348).

Thus, Drabble finds nothing lamentable about self-destructive or eccentric behavior if it follows from one's true nature. What she does deplore is the thwarting or deforming of this nature. Just as poor environmental conditions can impede the growth of a plant, so unhealthy familial and social conditions can deflect a person's proper development. Drabble fills her books with examples of this sad phenomenon. Simon Camish senses that his wife Julie's nature was perverted by her growing up in an unloving, philistine family: her natural sociability and love of pleasure were channeled into a desperate social climbing and materialism. He feels that "Julie had been made for a life so different, so much simpler" (*Needle's Eye*, p. 170), and it strikes him that a pleasant woman she befriends at a hotel on their vacation is "exactly what she herself could have been, had she not been so misled by false images: warm, fat, generous, amusing, immensely pleased by every drink she was offered, every course on the menu, everyone who spoke to her" (*Needle's Eye*, p. 183). Similarly, Clara Maugham's mother, who was intellectually and emotionally vibrant as a young girl, turns into a sour, dull woman as a result of a disappointing marriage and life in a narrow, provincial town. But some people, like some plants, are naturally tough and resilient, managing to combat the forces that threaten to thwart their proper development. Most of Drabble's protagonists are such people, and many of her plots involve these characters' attempts to discover their true natures and forge a life in accordance with them. Emma, temporarily lost and confused in her new role of wife and mother, is misled into believing herself to be a fragile romantic. But the experience of an extramarital affair ultimately helps her perceive her true self more accurately: "I became increasingly aware of my own strength, and of what a mistake I had made in trying to relapse into self-pity or the kind of romantic, self-centered indulgence that an affair with Wyndham had promised. These things had been against my nature," for the "truth was that I could survive anything, that I was made of cast-iron" (*Garrick Year*, p. 218).

Jane Gray's quest for her true nature is more complicated and elusive than Emma's. Although she, like most Drabble protagonists, believes that one's "nature [is] determinate, pre-eminent" (*Waterfall*, p. 55), she has tried to change her own. As a girl she sensed that she was capable of inordinate passion and selfishness, and so, out of a puritan obsession with guilt, she has tried to become innocent by living a renunciatory, reclusive, almost masochistic life, removing herself from all temptations and pleasures. But the temptation of an adulterous love affair rekindles the promptings of what she suspects to be her true nature: "I thought I could negate myself and wipe myself out. But when James looked at me it was my true self that he saw: alive, speaking, demanding him, despite all my efforts" (*Waterfall*, p. 59). She submits to these promptings, believing there "had been nothing else to do. There had never been a question of choice. There had been nothing in me capable of choosing. I had done what I had to do. I had done what my nature was, what I would have done anyway. I had done what was to be" (*Waterfall*, p. 183).

However, Jane, a poet obsessed with the discrepancy between language and the truth it attempts to express, finds it difficult to ascertain the truth about herself. She vacillates between thinking she was doomed to be unhappy and thinking she is capable of great joy, between the self-image of a fragile, romantic woman and that of a sturdy, practical one. The novel's elaborate structure and unusual narrative technique reflect her groping for the truth. The book is arranged in alternating third-person and first-person narrative sec-

tions. The former constitute Jane's fictional account of the affair and
the latter her nonfictional or more direct account. In the third-
person sections she usually presents herself as a miserable, neurotic
woman, on the verge of agoraphobia, and portrays the love affair in
a sublimely romantic light. But in the first-person sections she frequently becomes impatient with herself for having adopted that
view, regarding it as a method of escaping the truth and relinquish-
ing responsibility for adultery. She points out that in the third-
person narrative she has "deliberately exaggerated my helplessness,
my dislocation, as a plea for clemency. So that I should not be
judged. Poor helpless Jane, abandoned, afraid, timid, frigid, bereft"
(*Waterfall*, p. 275). She goes on, "I have to rethink it all, in terms of
what I now know myself to be. . . . Had I been destined for collapse,
I would have collapsed. But I was not" (*Waterfall*, p. 277). However,
she cannot rest for long with this assessment either: "And yet, that
can't be the whole truth. There are certain facts that remain, and I
turn back to them, not seeking extenuation, but seeking . . . the
truth" (*Waterfall*, p. 277).

These alternating perspectives continue throughout the novel.
Jane ceaselessly wonders whether the affair was meant to be or
whether it was an accident—whether she and James had met "in the
profound aspirations of their natures" or "in the shallow stretches of
ordinary weakness" (*Waterfall*, p. 248). She never finally attaches
herself to one, permanent view of her true nature and destiny. Her
complex narrative has been an attempt "to manage to find some kind
of unity," but she "seem[s] to be no nearer to it" (*Waterfall*, p. 250). In
this novel Drabble suggests both the importance of understanding
and following one's nature and the difficulty involved in ascertain-
ing exactly what this is.

Rose Vassiliou also faces difficulties in her attempt to live according to her true nature. Hers, however, arise not because of an inability to determine what it is but because of external circumstances—
societal, familial, legal, and economic—that threaten to prevent her
reaching her goal. She believes that she was meant to live a quiet,
modest, lower-class life, but she was born into the aristocracy and
inherited great wealth. She therefore has to battle to achieve the life
that suits her: she gives most of her money away to charity, divorces
her husband, who thinks she is mad for wanting to live in a blue-
collar neighborhood and send their children to state schools, and
braves the scorn and criticism of her parents and many of her
friends. But she achieves her goal and cherishes her hard-won way

of life. As she tells her new friend Simon Camish, while driving through the streets of her well-loved, run-down neighborhood, "All this, you see, I created it for myself. Stone by stone and step by step. I carved it out, I created it by faith, I believed in it, and then very slowly, it began to exist. And now it exists" (*Needle's Eye*, pp. 35-36). This life-style provides her with profound fulfillment and peace. However, her hold on it is tenuous: her husband will not leave her alone, alternately threatening to take the children away from her and begging her to have him back; she is constantly embroiled in lawsuits, ranging from divorce and child custody cases to legal snafus regarding her attempts to give her money away. In *The Needle's Eye* more than in any of her other novels, Drabble portrays the courage, difficulty, and loneliness that can be involved in living according to one's nature: "They had produced all kinds of arguments against [Rose], those hard realists with their central heating and their fitted carpets and their ambitions, and how could she persuade them that her life was as pleasant to her as a fitted carpet: to walk down the street, greeting this person here and this person there, to call in the sweet shop, the chemist, the greengrocer, the launderette . . . to do all these things was a pleasure to her, and a profound satisfaction" (*Needle's Eye*, pp. 146-47).

However, Drabble—and Rose—understand that there is no easy or right solution when individual nature and obligations to others are at odds. Christopher, Rose's husband, loves and wants the children as much as she does, and Rose is deeply pained to deprive him. Ultimately she chooses obligations to others over the needs of her nature: she takes Christopher back. But it has not been an easy choice and in doing so she deforms herself and thwarts her proper development: "She had ruined her own nature against her own judgment, for Christopher's sake, for the children's sake. She had sold for them her own soul" (*Needle's Eye*, p. 365).

Thus, although Drabble believes that it is important to obey the dictates of one's nature, she recognizes that there can be situations in which these impulses conflict with the needs of others. In such cases, one must decide which is the greater good—not always an easy decision, as Rose's tormented vacillations reveal. Family bonds, as we shall see in chapter 4, are, like individual nature, highly valued by Drabble. Usually her protagonists do not have to choose between these two, but in *The Needle's Eye* Drabble explores the difficulty of such a choice. Although she has Rose opt for the needs of others, she implies that this is a temporary situation. Rose's final words in the novel about the importance of weathering into identity suggest that eventually she will resume her old, more suitable life, perhaps after the children are grown. Drabble, then, believes that one should heed the exhortations of one's nature, but only insofar as these do not lead one to hurt or infringe on the rights of others.

II

A second sense in which Drabble employs the term nature is the biological composition of human beings. She likes to emphasize the physical side of people, reminding us that our identities are not entirely rooted in the mental, conscious part of ourselves. And just as she feels that people should submit to the promptings of their innate natures, so she also feels that they should respect their biological drives and processes. Many of her protagonists are highly cerebral people who gradually come to appreciate the physical aspect of themselves.

In the first three novels the development of maternal feelings causes the protagonists to recognize the force of primordial biological impulses. Although some feminist critics have been disturbed by the author's penchant for dwelling on the details of pregnancy, childbirth, nursing, and motherhood, Drabble is not endorsing these as women's sole function. Indeed, her women are strikingly intellectual and independent as well as maternal. She is certainly not subscribing to the image of the contented wife-mother promoted by traditional women's magazines. Instead, the maternal impulse is simply presented as one of the many reminders of our biological selves—one that Drabble herself, who was pregnant or rearing babies during the writing of her early novels, was experiencing at the time. Her argument is not for a return to the traditional female role but rather for a more balanced sense of identity, one that includes the biological as well as the cerebral sides of oneself.

In these early novels acknowledgment of their maternal impulses changes the way in which the protagonists perceive their identity and relationship to the world. Each protagonist moves toward a fuller understanding of herself by recognizing the nonrational, biological part of her identity. Sarah, the youngest and only non-mother of the three, is only half-aware of her buried maternal feelings; they surface a few times in the course of the novel, but she does not consciously register their significance. The first such time occurs in a shop when a small child starts patting Sarah's legs, apparently fascinated by her black stockings. This encounter affects her inordinately, and she cannot determine why: "I cannot say how strange and primitive those hands felt. My legs seemed to stir to life under them: they began to heave out of their usual torpor and to burn under me with an awful warning" (*Bird-Cage*, p. 183).

The second incident takes place when an acquaintance takes her to see his actress friend and her infant son in the actress' dressing room. Sarah is again strangely moved, and muses, "I shall never forget the way [the baby] lay there with its tiny curled fingers and its skin transparently blooming, a little pool of absolute stillness and silence in all the dirt and bustle" (*Bird-Cage*, pp. 193–94). These experiences seem to trigger Sarah's as yet dimly felt maternal impulses. Considered in the context of Drabble's work as a whole, the "awful warning" Sarah mentions would appear to refer to the maternal condition that awaits her, for the protagonists of later novels find themselves thoroughly immersed in this condition.

In her second and third novels Drabble suggests more directly the importance of maternal feelings, showing that those who experience the parent-child bond achieve a more fulfilling, natural way of life than those who do not. In *The Garrick Year* she implicitly contrasts the unsatisfactory, artificial existence of the theatre people who surround Emma to Emma's own more natural, instinctive existence, filled with maternal concerns and responsibilities. Although at first resenting the curtailed freedom of motherhood, Emma grows to appreciate the emotional depth and deeper satisfactions it provides. A flamboyant love affair with her actor husband's director—a misguided attempt at independence—causes her to realize that such behavior, which in bygone years she would have enjoyed, now leaves her unfulfilled. The experience of maternal love, with its weighty obligations and responsibilities, has made other, less committed types of relationships appear frivolous and shallow. The affair dies as Emma becomes increasingly uncomfortable in its dazed, unreal atmosphere. She sums up the change motherhood has wrought in her consciousness when she learns of the suicide of a sensitive, confused young actor friend: "Indecision drowned him. I used to be like Julian myself, but now I have two children, and you will not find me at the bottom of any river. I have grown into the earth, I am terrestrial" (*Garrick Year*, p. 219).

The change in consciousness of *The Millstone*'s protagonist is even more pronounced. Until her pregnancy, Rosamund has a very limited, rigid notion of her nature. Having always considered herself a cerebral, rational person, she runs her life in a highly organized fashion, allotting a certain amount of time to her work, at which she is very efficient and successful, and a certain amount to her social life. Uncomfortable with the emotional and physical side of existence, she has constructed an effective method whereby she can enjoy male companionship without sex: she dates two men simultaneously, allowing each to assume she sleeps with the other. However, her systematic approach to life disintegrates when she accidentally becomes pregnant the first time she sleeps with a man.

Although at first she sees only the negative side of her situation — "I was trapped in a human limit for the first time in my life, and I was going to have to learn how to live inside it" (*Millstone*, p. 65) — ultimately the pregnancy is responsible for her psychological and spiritual growth. It forces her to recognize that she is a biological as well as an intellectual creature. Gradually she develops a respectful awe of the side of herself she had formerly dismissed as "trivial things like the workings of my guts" (*Millstone*, p. 39). This change is reflected in her growing sense of kinship with the other women at the obstetrics-gynecology clinic, many of them poor and uneducated, with whom she has nothing in common except pregnancy: "Birth, pain, fear and hope, these were the subjects that drew us together in gloomy awe.... Indeed, so strong became the pull of nature that by the end of the six months' attendance I felt more in common with the ladies at the clinic than with my own acquaintances" (*Millstone*, p. 68).

Nearly all of Drabble's protagonists discover that submission to this "pull of nature" — their maternal instinct — is conducive to psychological well-being. It is a theme the author is reluctant to give up, even though the subjects of her recent novels — contemporary political and social problems and the anxieties of middle age — would not ordinarily lend themselves to it. She cannot resist including a pregnancy or a birth somewhere in these novels; for example, Anthony Keating's ex-wife is about to give birth to her fifth child at the age of thirty-eight, and Kate Armstrong accidentally becomes pregnant at the age of forty.

So important is the maternal role to Drabble's women that they are at a loss when they begin to move beyond the child-bearing age. Frances Wingate envies the female octopus, who dies once her maternal function has been fulfilled. Kate Armstrong suspects that her real, subconscious reason for stopping birth control — the conscious reason being her discovery that the pills had given her high blood pressure—was that she wanted another baby before it was too late. Even though tests show the fetus is severely deformed and her doctor urges her to have an abortion, she nearly decides to go through with the birth. In the end she does have an abortion, but she feels that in so doing she has wreaked serious damage to her psyche: "She had murdered [the baby]. For every good reason, she had murdered it. Maternity had been her passion, her primary passion in life, and she had been forced to deny it. Fate had forced her to undo her own nature. I denied my nature, thought Kate, therefore nature cannot help me. *Doing the right thing has destroyed me.* What shall I seek, what help from the unnatural? Or must I simply admit the violence done, the death of a soul? Her eyes filled with tears. There was no way out of this, it must be borne forever and ever, repeatedly" (*Middle Ground*, p. 235). Throughout the rest of the novel Kate continues to wonder whether the better choice would have been to succumb to maternal instinct and have the baby, no matter how deformed. Both protagonist and author are uncomfortable with the existential choices facing them in middle age—"the blank waste of freedom" (*Middle Ground*, p. 70)—and feel they have temporarily lost their footing now that the maternal role is being taken from them.[3]

In addition to stressing the importance of maternal instincts, Drabble further emphasizes the natural, biological aspect of human beings by frequent mention of flesh and blood and sex. Sarah describes the power primitive biological forces have over the individual: "In most people, and in myself, I am vaguely aware of a hinterland of nonpersonal action, where the pulls of sex and blood and society seem to drag me into unwilled motion, where the race takes over and the individual either loses himself in joy or is left helplessly self-regarding and appalled" (*Bird-Cage*, p. 78). Many of Drabble's characters develop an acute awareness of this flesh-and-blood part of their identity, some as a result of pregnancy, childbirth, and nursing, and some as a result of a sexual awakening.

Sexual feelings force Emma, who ordinarily regards herself as a highly rational, cerebral person, to recognize this other side of her identity. She recalls how perplexed and resistant she was the first time this awareness was thrust upon her, when she met her future husband: "I myself, the surface of me, felt calm . . . and the part of me that was not me but just any old thing, the inside of me, the blood and muscle and water and skin and bone of me, the rubbish, was blazing away, shuddering like some augur's sacrifice" (*Garrick Year*,

p. 28). She is similarly affected at a later stage of her life when she launches into an extramarital affair: "I wondered whether I was right to pay such attention to the part of me that responded with disturbing eagerness to the overtures of a man like Wyndham Farrar, for what was it that responded in this way but the physical rubbish of me, the blood and skin and so forth. . . . Because reason as I might, and as I did, it was this part, this dark and wanting part, that seemed to have reality, that seemed to tug and suck and pull at the rest of me with overriding need" (*Garrick Year*, p. 133).

For Jane Gray submission to the "dark and wanting part" that Emma describes effects psychological salvation. Previously neurotic and reclusive, she develops into a healthy, functioning human being as a result of a passionate love affair. The first time she experiences sexual desire she is amazed, for it springs from a part of herself she had not known existed: "That a desire so primitive could flow through her, unobstructed, like milk, astonished her" (*Waterfall*, p. 50). She gives herself over entirely to such feelings, to the extent that she is for a period of time inordinately obsessed with her passion. But ultimately this process proves to have been a necessary step in her journey to a fuller sense of identity.

Drabble's celebration of the flesh is perhaps best expressed through the reflections of Sarah Bennett: "what on earth was one to do about all this lovely body that one was obliged to walk around with? Skin and limbs and muscle, all glowing and hot with life and energy and hope?" She concludes, "Flesh is a straight gift" and "those who have got it had better make the most of this world" (*Bird-Cage*, p. 182).

But Drabble does not focus on only the joys of flesh; she also stresses its woes and vulnerabilities. Again, though, her purpose in so doing is to emphasize the physical component of human identity. An inordinate number of physical injuries and accidents take place or are discussed in Drabble's novels. For example, in *The Middle Ground* while Evelyn Stennett lies in the emergency room after being badly burned, her children and Kate Armstrong sit around the Stennett living room reminiscing about the various gruesome accidents they all have had. Many of Drabble's married couples engage in violent physical fights, and detailed descriptions are given of the blood that flows in these battles. For example, in *The Needle's Eye* Rose steps by mistake on the broken ketchup bottle her husband has hurled at her in a tempestuous argument and cuts "her foot, a curious cut between the toes, God knows how it had happened but it bled like nothing on earth, and what with the blood and ketchup and the damp chips trodden into the carpet she had wished to die" (*Needle's Eye*, p. 81).

Drabble is evidently fascinated by this type of bloody domestic spectacle for she creates strikingly similar episodes in other novels. In *The Realms of Gold* a battle between Joy Schmidt and her husband's lover, Frances, results in "earth [from overturned potted plants] all over the carpet, as well as wine and blood and glass" (*Realms*, p. 72). And in *The Garrick Year* Emma, distracted and upset by the current disastrous state of her marriage, accidentally drops a bottle of milk on the kitchen floor. Trying to clean up the mess while at the same time fighting back tears and keeping an eye on her toddler daughter, she cuts herself and begins to bleed, becoming "damp with milk and blood and tears, a varied sea of grief" (*Garrick Year*, pp. 189–90).

As these scenes indicate, crises in the characters' lives often result in or are accompanied by a physical disintegration—usually wounds and cuts. The blood serves to remind characters that they are, after all, merely biological organisms. This realization is often a check against a character's taking his or her psychological or existential problems too seriously, as when Kate Armstrong is jolted out of a Proustian exploration of her psyche by the intruding awareness of aches and pains in her feet.

Although Drabble often displays the woes of physical existence, she nonetheless appreciates and is in awe of this side of human life. To her, even those biological processes that are usually considered undesirable should be submitted to. Indeed, she regards the sight of physical human aging, weathering, and decaying as aesthetically pleasing. In loving detail she describes the etched lines around her middle-aged characters' eyes, the dry, wrinkled skin of their hands, their liver-colored "age" spots, their prominent veins. A favorite word of hers is "weathered." For example, Karel Schmidt muses affectionately on the appearance of his lover, Frances: "[her skin] had been weathered, as she was fond of pointing out, by sun and sand, like an ancient monument. She was covered in blemishes: scars, rough patches, corns, permanently damaged nails, moles" (*Realms*, p. 92). And perhaps Drabble's most powerful statement of her appreciation of human weathering is her description of Rose Vassiliou's friend Emily:

> Emily had grown so beautiful over the years that it was now almost unbearable, one could hardly bear to gaze at her, so

moving were the marks of time and beauty. Her hair had streaked, had turned grey and white: it was thick and heavy, she wore it untidily pinned up, a brown pin holding it, coarse and drooping, sinking from the pin with the weight of years, and her skin, once brown and sallow, had faded and whitened, her lips were almost blue, so had the pink retreated, her eyes were etched in red and blue lines of amazing splendour, her whole face was lined and carved and withered into beauty, her hands too were marked with age, their veins courageously upstanding, their nails blue with a fine withdrawal. She seemed the image of time, triumphant, vindicated, conquering but conquered. (*Needle's Eye*, p. 360)

The cumulative effect of Drabble's concentration on human physicality and its cycles is an impression of the human being as intimately sharing in the biological processes and drives that comprise all nature. Jane Gray's observation "So liquid we are, inside our stiff bodies, so easily resolved to other elements" (*Waterfall*, p. 229) aptly captures the author's perspective. Drabble is not, however, an antirationalist; it is simply that she, like D. H. Lawrence, believes that occasional recognition of the primitive, biological part of our identity is an antidote to the modern disease of alienation and extreme self-consciousness. Most of her protagonists, like herself, are far too involved in the practical, day-to-day business of living to be constantly dissolving into their primitive roles or to concentrate wholly on the flesh-and-blood aspect of their identities. However, her novels play up this perspective because she believes it is important to remember that the conscious, intellectual view of ourselves is not the whole picture.

III

The third form of nature which Drabble addresses is the natural physical world outside human beings—the earth, its vegetation, and its elements. Just as she emphasizes the biological aspect of human identity, so she also believes it is important for people to understand their essential connection with the natural physical world. She reveals her own attitude and concerns when, in her essay on Thomas Hardy, she praises as his greatest achievement the fictional recreation of an Edenic situation in which "the whole of the natural world has a strong organic unity, which he apprehends at times with a mystical clarity: borderlines are blurred, and man becomes part of nature."[4] Like Hardy, she perceives the "ancient unbroken sympathy between man and the creation,"[5] and knows that "modern man may cut himself off by thought and aspiration from the world he grew from, but essentially man's history hitherto has been one of infinitely slow change, where the animate and the inanimate were part of the same large slow pattern."[6] Though not to the extent that Hardy does, Drabble also draws her characters against this pattern, frequently minimizing their distinctly human features and highlighting those they share with the rest of physical nature.

She achieves this effect primarily through her use of vegetation and elemental imagery. In her novels the natural world is always associated with spiritual and psychological well-being. In *A Summer Bird-Cage* Sarah expresses her desire for a rich, fulfilling existence with the metaphor "I should like to bear leaves and flowers and fruit" (*Bird-Cage*, p. 77). And when feeling aimless and anxious about her life, she reflects, "the seasons had a lovely rhythm and I had none at all" (*Bird-Cage*, p, 60). In *The Garrick Year* Emma's growth involves both an acceptance of her maternal instincts, as has been shown, and a deepening appreciation of the natural world. Early in the novel she is horrified when she learns of her impending stay in the countryside with her husband's acting troupe. But once there she gradually changes her view. Exposure to natural scenery causes her to perceive the artificial, tawdry quality of her own life. One night, walking home from a theatre party that has filled her with disgust, she spots a swan floating downstream on the river, and "the tranquillity of the image, compared with the smoky heat that [she] had left, filled [her] with hopelessness" (*Garrick Year*, p. 142). Her sense of nature's importance develops further on an outing in the country with her lover: "Here I was, in the midst of all the greenery that I had mocked with my friends in London, and I was unnerved by it. It seemed more real than London, the river and the trees and the grass, so much profusion, so much of everything, and not a human in reach" (*Garrick Year*, p. 148). Finding an old, rotten apple on the ground, she reflects, "this was the course of nature, for apples to fall off trees and lie in the grass, and . . . the other thing, the thing with which I was familiar, the picking and the eating and the selling, was a much later development" (*Garrick Year*, p. 114).

In later novels Drabble weaves the vegetation imagery more elaborately into the overall structures. A sustained analogy between human beings and plants is the governing metaphor of *Jerusalem the*

Golden, creating the theme that people, like plants, should develop in a natural, unobstructed way, in their native soil and climate. The protagonist, Clara, is dissatisfied with the "barren," "infertile" (*Jerusalem*, p. 33) soil—a repressive, provincial Methodist family—in which she was reared, and attempts to "transplant" herself by moving to London and adopting a totally different way of life. But in Drabble's world the tie with one's roots is so basic that Clara cannot get away psychologically. She obsessively fears that if she lets her will relax she will end up drifting into old family patterns and attitudes: "I am chased, I am pursued, I run and run, but I will never get away, the apple does not fall far from the tree" (*Jerusalem*, p. 193).

The book is a study of the pernicious effects of attempting a radical severance from and denial of one's background. In striving to live on will alone, Clara turns into a monstrous figure. With a calculating eye, she selects her friends and acquaintances according to their ability to provide her with the rich, exciting existence she is after. In keeping with her unnatural attitude, she sleeps with men not out of sexual or emotional need but out of a desire for intrigue—for this reason she particularly likes affairs with married men. So warped are her values that she regards as the height of achievement her newly attained status of kept mistress of the glamorous Gabriel Denham, ignoring the fact that she does not love him and that the affair is creating problems in his marriage and family life. Ironically, she regards her new way of life as healthy, applauding herself for having "done to herself what she had been trying for years to do to herself: she had cut herself off forever, and she could drift now, a flower cut off from its root, or a seed perhaps, an airy seed dislodged, she could drift now without fear of settling ever again upon the earth" (*Jerusalem*, p. 220).

Clara's deludedness and unnaturalness are further revealed by her attitude toward the Denhams, the wealthy, artistic family—the antithesis of her own—she befriends in London. Whereas Clara is consumed with awe and admiration of the Denhams, labelling them "the real thing" (*Jerusalem*, p. 115), Drabble implies that their style is artificial and studied. For example, their home is elaborately decorated with mirrors everywhere, suggesting their vanity and need for an audience (which they find in Clara); there is a golden eagle on a piece of furniture; instead of growing plants and flowers, they fill their garden with sculptures and urns. Indeed, Clara grows accustomed to leaving their house with the feeling of having strenuously applied her attention to "works of art arranged in some peculiarly absorbing art gallery" (*Jerusalem*, p. 126). Although she perceives as laudable the Denhams' absorption in the complexities and intricacies of their family relationships, it may well strike the reader as self-centered and decadent. In fact, the life of intrigue and emotional complication Clara is after, if stripped of the glamour with which she clothes it, is nothing more than the stuff of soap opera. Although Drabble implies that it is dangerous to sever one's roots and live by sheer will, she sympathizes with Clara's desire to do so, for the family Clara has grown up in is indeed stultifying. This is suggested by, among other things, the reluctant, perfunctory way they tend their garden. And, as has been pointed out in an earlier section, Drabble is distressed by the fact that unhealthy home conditions can blight the development of a child. Therefore, Clara's course of action is understandable. However, Drabble feels it is necessary to come to terms with one's background and accept it as part of oneself, no matter how undesirable it is. Although she does not have Clara mend her ways and return to the family fold, she does have her finally accept her connection with her past, as shall be demonstrated in the chapter on family.

In *The Waterfall* Drabble expands her vegetation imagery to include an elaborate water motif. In particular, water is a symbol of the sexual passion that is the means to the protagonist's salvation. At the novel's opening Jane is sexually, emotionally, and intellectually dry. A sudden affair with her cousin's husband, James Otford, awakens her passion and ultimately restores her desire to go on living and working. The waterfall of the title has a triple reference. It refers to the dazzling card trick of that name that James performs for Jane and therefore symbolizes the magical power he—and their love— have over her. It also refers to the actual waterfall they visit at the end of the novel, an excursion that combines the sublime and the humorous, qualities that eventually prove characteristic of their relationship once the early phase of high romance is over. But on the most significant level the title refers to Jane's first experience of orgasm, which she describes in a way that conjures up a picture of a waterfall: she feels at first "alone and high up, stranded, unable to fall: and then suddenly but slowly, for the first time ever, just as she thought she must die without him forever, she started to fall, painfully, anguished, but falling at last, falling, coming towards him, meeting him at last, down there in his arms, half dead but not dead, crying out to him, trembling, shuddering, quaking, drenched and drowned, down there at last in the water, not high in her lonely place" (*Waterfall*, pp. 180–81).

Just as orgasm is the central experience of Jane and James' relationship, so the waterfall is the central image of the novel. And the waters from this waterfall, so to speak, flow through the rest of the book in the same way that sexual passion informs every aspect of the lovers' relationship. The narrative, told by Jane, a poet highly conscious of imagery, is replete with references to water. She often refers to her condition prior to the love affair as "dry," "ossified," "petrified," and "dusty." She uses water imagery to describe their lovemaking and the beneficial effects of their relationship. In a typical passage she declares that she and James were "parched and starving" before they met, but when they began to love,

> the water that [they] drank, the so much longed for water, was sweet, not sour and brackish to the taste. Nor were the leaves green merely through the glamour of distance, through the contrast with the preceding waste: they remained green to the touch, dense, endless foresting boughs, an undiscovered country, no shallow quickly-exhausted, quickly-drained sour well, but miles of verdure, rivers, fishes, coloured birds, miles with no sign of ending, and, perhaps, beyond them all, no ending but the illimitable, circular, inexhaustible sea. (*Waterfall*, p. 252)

In addition to references to water, the novel is pervaded with other images of earthy liquidity. The bed Jane and James make love in is always damp with their bodily moistures; Jane's milk spills on the sheets when she is nursing the baby; Jane weeps tears of joy during orgasm. The novel is filled with allusions to natural liquids, which contribute to the water-as-nourisher motif.

Again in *The Needle's Eye*, plants and vegetation frequently work as objective correlatives for the good life. When we first meet Simon Camish, he is embittered, stuck in a joyless, sterile existence. His background and his mother are remarkably similar to Clara Maugham's, and like the Maughams, the Camishes did not enjoy gardening. Therefore, his sudden inspiration, the night after he meets Rose Vassiliou, to go out into his garden in the winter moonlight signals the beginning of his spiritual growth. The fact that there is hope for him, that he is not emotionally dead, is symbolized by his tentative respect for nature: "He did not know the names of [the plants], but he stood carefully, on the earthy border, so that they should not be crushed" (*Needle's Eye*, p. 69). And there is the symbolic suggestion that a spiritual rebirth is in store for him: "A perpetual winter was what he expected: he would, he felt, experience no surprise should, one spring, the trees refuse to bud, and the flowers to blossom. Why should those branches not remain for ever bare, the earth for ever hard and inhospitable? By what grace did these green hopes and gentle exhalations perpetually recur? He had done nothing to deserve so munificent a resurgence" (*Needle's Eye*, p. 70).

It is, in fact, Rose's naturalness—her lined face, undisguised by cosmetics; her well-worn clothes; her shabby, weathered home—that appeals to him. Having grown disgusted with the hypocrisy and materialism of the smart society he moves in, he sees in Rose's life the possibility of salvation. The fact that his posh acquaintances fill their homes with plants strikes him as incongruous, for their lives are so artificial. Rose, however, he regards as very much a part of nature. He refers to "the soft, full lake of her nature" (*Needle's Eye*, p. 175) and compares its emanations with those of "the dawn, or other natural manifestations of the self-sufficient natural world" (*Needle's Eye*, p. 175).

As Simon goes through a spiritual rebirth in the course of the novel, he begins to develop a greater interest in nature and vegetation. He spends time working in his garden. He takes his small daughter on a long nature walk, which proves to be the beginning of a breakthrough in his relationship with his family, leading him to try to relate better to his children and his wife, from whom he has long been emotionally estranged.

In *The Realms of Gold*, too, natural scenery and vegetation are linked with psychological and spiritual health. The novel on the surface is a story about contemporary, sophisticated, urban people. They jet to other continents, attend international conventions, discuss Freud. At the center is a uniquely modern woman: Frances Wingate, highly independent and capable, a successful scholar and archaeologist, divorced and raising a large family on her own. However, this modern scene is presented against the symbolic backdrop of an older, more primitive world. John Updike aptly observes of the novel, "The conversations, the dinner parties, the conferences (all trendy, flirtatious, and desultory) feel superficial, perhaps because they appear so to the author—a crust over the earthy realities."[7]

In this novel Drabble implies that modern life is not very far removed from an ancient time when nature was more apparent and abundant, playing a greater role in one's immediate consciousness. She presents her characters in an evolutionary light. Although Frances is a thoroughly modern woman, she is also merely the latest link in a biological chain that stretches back to primitive times, a chain that seems to be tugging her backwards during the course of the novel. An accumulation of mud and amphibian imagery contributes to this impression. As a girl, Frances spent long hours lying on her stomach in a muddy ditch studying its flora and fauna, a memory to which she frequently returns. She and her lover, Karel, gravitate toward ditches, make love in the mud, and are profoundly awed and delighted by their discovery of a "chorus" of hundreds of frogs honking in an old drainpipe. Frances says of these frogs, "A natural product of the landscape, they were" (*Realms*, pp. 19–20), an observation she has also made about her own ancestors.

A primitive, Edenic life haunts and pulls at her as well as many of the other characters. In an emblematic scene, Frances tramps through the mud and thistles to visit the uninhabited rural cottage of her late great-aunt. Sitting on the dank, mossy stone floor of the cottage, with creepers and brambles and roses growing in through the windows and under the doors, she is filled with awe and realizes she wants to live there. Despite the decay, Frances views the house favorably: "Nature had gently enfolded it, had embraced it and taken it and thicketed it in, with many thorns and briars; nature had wanted it, and not rejected it" (*Realms*, p. 299). Similarly, nature draws back to itself other members of her extended family. David Ollerenshaw, who believes that "man [is] merely another agent of natural weathering and change, like wind and water" (*Realms*, p. 179), spends much time on solitary outings in places relatively untouched by human beings, such as northern Scotland and the Sahara. Stephen Ollerenshaw goes out to the forest to commit suicide, covering himself with tree roots. Hugh and Natasha Ollerenshaw, desiring a more natural way of life, move to a country cottage, where Natasha gardens, bakes bread, and shuns modern appliances, and Hugh chops wood and builds fires. For all these characters, immersion in nature is a way of mitigating the anxieties of modern life.

The same is true for certain characters in *The Ice Age*. Just as Frances Wingate is a prototypical modern woman, Anthony Keating is a prototypical modern man—agnostic, addicted to the fast pace of city life, obsessed with making money, and dependent on alcohol to relieve his tensions. But a sudden series of economic and physical reversals forces him to change his life-style. He moves to the country and gives up alcohol, cigarettes, and rich food. Although at first lost and numb in such an existence, he gradually goes through a profound spiritual change, in which he shifts his rhythms to harmonize with nature's. He reeducates his palate so as not to need gross and violent stimulants, and learns to be fulfilled by nature's simple pleasures. Drabble expresses her bleakest views in this novel, emphasizing the prevalence of disaster and destruction in life and giving the characters very little control over these forces. Nonetheless, she implies, there is a haven of sorts from them: if one identifies more closely with nature, one is less disturbed by worldly reversals, for nature is eternally renewable. As the omniscient narrator points out while Anthony lies in bed reflecting on the fickleness of fortune and the relentlessness of destruction, "A thrush sang in the apple tree in the garden, despite this" (*Ice Age*, p. 245).

In *The Middle Ground* the vegetation imagery is scanty but significant. The novel's landscape is urban London and the protagonist is very much of a city woman, absorbed in a bustling journalism career with a London newspaper. But at age forty Kate suddenly finds herself in a "peculiar draughty open space" (*Middle Ground*, p. 13), cut off from her past and unsure about her future. Depressed, she wonders, "How can one regain one's feeling for life?" (*Middle Ground*, p. 73).

Both Kate's despair and her gradual recovery are suggested in part by her changing attitudes toward nature. At one of her lowest points she labels as "sinister" the intense vegetative smell emanating from a garden she passes by, and in distraction she nearly treads on a dead pigeon lying on the pavement. During this period of her life, she reflects that her ability to love seems to have "sunk into some cold wintry hibernating part of herself. It wasn't dead, she told herself, it couldn't be dead, perhaps it was just waiting for some kind of spring, perhaps it would wake up and blossom again?" (*Middle Ground*, p. 63).

When hope begins to stir in her, she again chooses nature imagery to describe her outlook. For example, in a moment of buoyancy at a dinner party, she suddenly observes to herself that life "is fun. After all. Or at least, bits of it are. The trees in the square outside were full of new green leaves. What could go wrong?" (*Middle Ground*, p. 44). Another time, looking out a train window, she notices how nature can force its way into even an inhospitable industrial environment: "She gazed out of the window at high brick walls, at buildings and building sites, at the backs of factories, at tufts of greenery and ragged yellow flowers clinging boldly to stony niches" (*Middle Ground*, p. 108).

Observations like the latter, reminding one of the preeminence of nature, are always salutary for Drabble's characters in that they help them put their existential problems into perspective. Kate's gradual overcoming of despair is in part accomplished by her recognition of the supremacy and soothing power of nature. A trip back to her childhood London neighborhood on a journalistic assignment becomes the occasion for many such insights and launches Kate on the path to psychological recovery. On the train ride to Romley she recalls what a hot autumn it has been and speculates, "Perhaps the sun shone so brightly to remind her that, whatever she thought of it, it was still there. She couldn't ruin it or blot it out with the dull disk of herself. If she fell silent forever, it would continue to shine" (*Middle Ground*, p. 109).

Once back in the old neighborhood she is struck by many reminders of nature's power. Although Romley has become a morass of concrete "fly-overs and underpasses and unfinished supports" (*Middle Ground*, p. 112), and an artificial lake and pleasure garden have been constructed, primitive nature intrudes here and there in the form of "brambles and bushes and long grass," "bushes [that] were laden with berries," "[a] crabapple dazzling with pale-orange glowing fruits," and "[trails] of old man's beard and traveller's joy silver[ing] the scrub" (*Middle Ground*, pp. 113–14). But the most important sign of nature is the neighborhood's grass-covered sewage embankment. This is one of the novel's central images, serving much the same purpose for Kate that the Tockley ditch in *The Realms of Gold* serves for Frances Wingate: a complex symbol of the protagonist's connection with the primitive natural world, with her childhood, and with her buried, "real" self.

As a city child, Kate had been fascinated by the embankment, "a green spine through the surrounding brick industrial wilderness, a link with scrubby open space which counted, to the children of the district, as countryside" (*Middle Ground*, p. 18). She loved to "lie on her belly and press her face against the grating and inhale" the organic, vegetable smell (*Middle Ground*, p. 116), much as Frances used to lie face down in her ditch watching water beetles. Walking along the bank again as an adult, Kate reexperiences many of her childhood sensations, and thus the bank serves as an entryway into her buried, childhood self, symbolized by the underground network of drains and pipes and their "powerful and secret" smell (*Middle Ground*, p. 116). Kate's psychological journey into her childhood is an attempt to bridge the gap between her "underground" self and her "conscious," "daylight self" (*Middle Ground*, p. 118). Drabble then goes on to compare this kind of integrated self with a plant having "dirty, tangled roots. . . . Impacted, interwoven, scrubby, interlocked, fibrous, cankerous, tuberous, matted, ancient, matted" (*Middle Ground*, p. 132). Conversely, the dislocated identity which Kate has until now been experiencing is symbolized by the "artificial pleasure ground," in which "dear, solitary, carefully nurtured groups of saplings stood and shivered in their loneliness, straight and slim, sad and forlorn. Their roots in artificial loam, reared in artificial fibre pots, carefully separate. Tastefully arranged, fruitlessly deployed" (*Middle Ground*, p. 132).

Natural imagery thus serves both as a reminder to Kate of her proper place in the scheme of things and as a metaphor for the healthy, integrated psyche. The novel ends with an image that accomplishes this dual purpose. Kate purchases a potted tree that she plans eventually to plant in her backyard. She wants "a tree that will outlive [her]" (*Middle Ground*, p. 272), whose presence will be a constant reminder of the preeminence of nature. At the same time, the tree is a metaphor for Kate's own psyche: "a hardy tree" (*Middle Ground*, p. 272), which can withstand a temporary stay in an artificial environment (Kate says, "it has to go in the back garden, really it isn't supposed to live in the house, but a few days won't kill it" [*Middle Ground*, p. 272]).

According to Drabble, then, spiritual health lies in part in remembering that one is an integral part of the natural physical world. Indeed, her recent work of nonfiction, *A Writer's Britain* (1979), has as its thesis the idea that people, writers and artists in particular, possess a deep sense of connection with their native landscapes. In this light she analyzes the impact of the Romantics:

> I am beginning to think that one of the reasons why Wordsworth struck so deep a response is that he was drawing on deep sources of collective feeling, on a primitive animistic view of the world, certainly present in earlier times, but powerfully suppressed by the scientific seventeenth and eighteenth centuries. The child and peasant see inanimate objects and natural forces as possessed of a life of their own. Wordsworth was able, like Freud in later days, to restore an

essential contact with the primitive, to divine its workings, and to restore an earlier vision. Man, cut off from nature by centuries of rationalism, was restored to her bosom.[8]

In her emphases, both on man's essential connection with the physical world and on the biological side of human identity, discussed in the preceding section, Drabble aligns herself with the tradition of what John Alcorn has termed the "naturist novel." The naturists were a school of modern writers, fathered by Hardy and Lawrence, who viewed the human being as primarily part of an animal and geological continuum, believing that biology can be a source of psychic health and of moral authority. They claimed that wisdom derives not from theories but "from the quieter and more enduring geological truth hidden within Egdon Heath, the Marabar Caves, the Arabian deserts, and the Amazonian jungles."[9] In nature lies hope, an attitude which sets the naturist novelist apart from the twentieth-century novelist of existential despair. Although Drabble does not shun intellectual or moral authority as guides for modern behavior, she sides with the naturists in the view that contemporary people have lost sight of their intimate connection with the biological and physical worlds and that they must regain a sense of this bond.

IV

Be it in the form of individual temperament, biological processes, or the natural physical world, Drabble believes that nature must be respected and submitted to. And for the most part she advocates passive submission, as practiced by Rose, who allows herself to weather physically without interference, and Frances and Jane, who do not use birth control because they believe in letting nature take its course. Jane's respect for the organic is so intense that she allows her bread to go stale: "I think it's immoral to impede the course of nature by a tin lid. I mean to say, if things are made to go stale, it hardly seems right to stop them, does it?" (*Waterfall*, p. 173). And she empathizes with a schoolboy who refuses to interfere with nature by cutting his hair or fingernails.

But occasionally Drabble displays a different attitude toward the human being's relationship with nature. While she admires plain, shabby, natural Rose, she is also attracted to those who help nature along—lush, made-up Sophy Brent (*Garrick Year*); glamorous clothes-horse Louise Bennett (*Bird-Cage*); and flashy, materialistic

Len Wincobank (*Ice Age*). This attraction is not inconsistent with her love of the natural; it simply reflects another way of regarding nature—nature as a source of gifts to be cultivated by human beings. For example, if one has been given physical beauty, one should appreciate and make the most of it. She puts this view into the mouth of Louise Bennett, who justifies her indulgence in beautiful clothes by arguing that her appearance involves "paying a debt to nature" (*Bird-Cage*, p. 212). Similarly, describing Alison Murray's physical charms as "gifts" (*Ice Age*, p. 33), Drabble lauds her attempts to retain her beauty and prevent herself from growing fat, gray, and wrinkled. As Valerie Myer points out, Drabble feels that the gifts of nature—beauty, intellect, talent, wealth—are to be "used and enjoyed, not thwarted and denied," for when "the body is bruised to pleasure soul, nature is frustrated in its purposes and potentialities."[10] She creates many appealing portraits of people who derive deep pleasure from their gifts. Their pleasure is a way of paying homage to nature.

Drabble thus approves of Frances Wingate, who delights in her many career accomplishments, reflecting with satisfaction, "I stole all that from nature and got it for myself" (*Realms*, p. 24). Two of her most lovable characters are *The Ice Age*'s Maureen Kirby and Len Wincobank, whose pleasure in their material riches is both profound and innocently child-like. Having grown up in working-class slums, they cannot get over their good fortune at finding themselves affluent in their early thirties, and their delight in sumptuous dinners, posh hotels, and fancy cars never diminishes. Sitting in bed watching television in a hotel room, consuming elegant room-service sandwiches and drinks, is their idea of "paradise" (*Ice Age*, p. 86). Rather than regard such an attitude as shallow, Drabble admires the zest and appreciation with which they take advantage of the gift of wealth. With great sympathy she describes how Len as a boy "appreciated every blessing of the material life" that his impoverished family managed to achieve: "Every little luxury Len had enjoyed, admired, and as he and his brothers started to work, began to bring home pay packets, how miraculously easy and warm life had become, with a hired television set, a new radiogram, and even, finally, a telephone" (*Ice Age*, p. 125).

Drabble defends her views on the right use of wealth in her biography of Arnold Bennett, whose background was very similar to Len Wincobank's and after whom she possibly modelled this character. Countering the accusations of Virginia Woolf and others who regarded Bennett as crass and materialistic, she argues that although it is "easy to laugh at Bennett's enthusiasm for the modern and the grand," there is "something very infectious and very sound in his admiration. He came from a world where badly paid skivvies spent entire lifetimes on their hands and knees scrubbing floors and steps, and living in cold damp basements. Why not hail the vacuum cleaner, central heating, washing machines?"[11] She is touched by his profound delight in his fancy yacht and automobile and his expensive home. His attitude was composed of appreciation and awe rather than voracity or self-congratulation. Such an attitude, which many of Drabble's fortunate characters possess, implies that they realize, as Bennett did, that one's riches, talents, or physical attributes are gifts of nature and as such should be respected.

Drabble holds a submissive attitude toward the natural realm as well as toward the metaphysical. Although such submission means that one is not a free agent, there is solace to be found in such a position. Awareness of the power and importance of nature in one's life can mitigate the existential anxiety that frequently overcomes contemporary people. Drabble's characters gain comfort and strength whenever they experience this awareness.

In holding such an attitude and in creating a fictional world which embodies it, Drabble demonstrates her departure from the prevailing twentieth-century attitude of alienation. In *The Mysteries of Identity* (1977), Robert Langbaum argues that our current obsession with and anxiety about identity has its roots in the Enlightenment, which dissolved the notion of God-created values and God-created souls. Much modern literature—most notably that of Arnold, Eliot, and Beckett—reflects this dissolution, positing a self unable to connect with anything outside itself. Langbaum points out that certain writers have responded to this situation by adopting philosophies that enable them to bridge the gap: Wordsworth with his theory of the individual as part of nature, Lawrence with his belief in knowledge and salvation through sex.[12] Drabble would do well as another example. Through her marked affinity with older attitudes and sensibilities regarding metaphysics and nature, she holds up in her fiction an alternative to the modern person's existential alienation.

4

Family and the Individual

Family, like nature, is in Drabble's fictional world an important factor in a person's identity as well as a source of spiritual and psychological solace. Although the family curtails individual freedom, by influencing one's character and imposing familial responsibilities, it is ultimately a bulwark against life's turbulence and uncertainties. Many of her protagonists move from rejection to at least partial acceptance of their families, both by recognizing their own inheritance of certain ancestral traits and by assuming greater responsibility toward their relatives. Family, then, is another one of the conditions of existence, along with metaphysical and natural forces, before which human beings must bow. The movement in Drabble's novels is always away from existential protest toward graceful submission to these conditions.

Drabble often adopts the perspective of the individual as being merely a link in a family chain. The force of family background is such that her characters sometimes marvel at the difference between their own and their ancestors' lives. However, they suspect that it was only an accident of fate that caused this aberration and that if left to a natural course they would have been formed in the family mold. Clara, whose previously quoted statement "the apple does not fall far from the tree" (*Jerusalem*, p. 193) sums up this suspicion, reflects that but for "Battersby Grammar School and the welfare state and Gabriel Denham and the course of time" (*Jerusalem*, p. 228) she would have developed along the same lines as her mother. Frances Wingate makes a similar observation: "One cannot escape one's destiny. And one day, in a moment of comic horror, it had occurred to her that in seeking to avoid her mother's ghost, she had in fact behaved exactly like her mother." She concludes that "but for Karel, she would have ended up like her mother" (*Realms*, p. 81).

This remark echoes Drabble's own words in a recent interview: "It's as though there's an ancestral ghost haunting the family. I hear myself saying things that my grandmother used to say."[1] Frances also reflects, while perusing records of her family past, that "out of this darkness, her father had clambered, oddly gifted, oddly persevering, a freak escape" (*Realms*, p. 300). She suspects that but for her father's driving ambition, she would be living the provincial rural life of her ancestors.

Drabble thus leans toward an evolutionary view of the individual, believing that people are not as far removed from their ancestral pasts as they usually think. This notion is touched on in most of her novels, but only in *The Realms of Gold* does it become a prominent theme. It has already been pointed out, in the discussion of the natural physical world, how the mud, amphibian, and vegetation imagery contributes to an evolutionary perspective of the protagonist. The archaeological and anthropological imagery also contributes to this effect. Throughout the book a parallel is drawn between the contemporary and the ancient. Because three of the main characters, Frances, Karel, and David, are, respectively, an archaeologist, an historian, and a geologist, there is much discussion of and emphasis on the past. And therefore the subject of this book, Frances' extended family, is presented in an anthropological perspective.

In the novel a kind of double vision emerges, in which characters and their actions are presented simultaneously as both contemporary and archetypal phenomena. For example, although Frances, a divorced, liberated woman, juggling career and family responsibilities, is in one respect a product of the modern era, she is also merely a modern variation of an ancient type—the matriarch of a primitive tribe. Her brother, Hugh, gazing at her one evening as she sits in front of the fire at his cottage, is suddenly struck by her resemblance to a picture of Queen Boadicea in their childhood book *Historical Pictures Through the Ages*: "It came to him so vividly, and he could see that she too remembered—Boadicea, Queen of the Iceni, sitting in her hut contemplating the overthrow of the Romans. She was staring into the peat fire, much as Frances was staring now, a goblet of wine at her elbow, a skin map spread on the floor at her feet" (*Realms*, p. 201). Frances even carries her lover's old pair of false teeth around as a keepsake, much as primitives invested certain objects with ritual significance.

The ancient nature of contemporary customs and rituals is continually emphasized. The narrator explains both Janet Bird's and Frances Wingate's marriages from an anthropological point of view, describing how each of them had become infected with the prenuptial mania of wedding presents as a way of avoiding their fears and doubts about marriage: "There is some tribal insanity that comes over women, as they approach marriage: society offers Pyrex dishes and silver teaspoons as bribes, as bargains, as anesthesia against self-sacrifice. Stuck about with silver forks and new carving knives, as in a form of acupuncture, the woman lays herself upon the altar, upon the couch, half numb" (*Realms*, p. 125).

Another example of this yoking together of past and present is the dinner party Janet Bird and her husband give in their modern suburban home. The evening gradually takes on a primitive tone when the electricity goes off and the three couples huddle around the candlelight trying to get a gas camping stove to heat coffee. Playfully, they begin to ruminate on the archaeological spectacle they present. One of them suggests, "Let's just sit here quietly until we freeze to death. They'll find us in the morning, dressed in our best. We could be put in a museum as a diorama, they could call it 'Dinner Party in the Provinces in the Nineteen Seventies.' They could transport your entire lounge to Tockley Museum and set it down as the next one on from all those Roman relics and bits of agricultural machinery, Janet. And I bet you people would look at it in a hundred years or two, and say, oh, look, isn't that nice, oh, I do wish I'd lived *then*" (*Realms*, p. 163).

Drabble frequently invokes this kind of perspective, which simultaneously causes the present to appear in an historical light and the past to seem closer. It also places the contemporary individual in the context of a cultural and tribal network stretching back in time. The characters, sometimes consciously but usually subconsciously, are powerfully attracted to this web. Frances, in mid-life mysteriously moved to pay a visit to her ancestral home, muses, "The eels go back to the same beds, the swallows fly south in the summer. And [I] had gone back for a weekend to the flat Midlands. What had [I] found there? What held [me] like a stone around [my] neck?" (*Realms*, p. 188).[2] And when Janet Bird suddenly decides to take her new baby to visit an aged great-aunt whom she has never met, she feels that in so doing she is obeying "some primitive edict of some long disrupted kinship network" (*Realms*, p. 279).

In *The Realms of Gold* Drabble demonstrates the individual's connection not only with his ancestry but also with his living, extended family. She effects this primarily through her narrative technique. An intrusive, omniscient narrator ranges freely across the wide canvas of characters, pointing out the similarities between various Ollerenshaw family members. Often in the midst of her narrative about one character Drabble will insert a parenthetical sentence or paragraph telling us what a relative hundreds of miles away is doing at the same moment. Throughout the bulk of the novel many of these relatives are unaware of the others' existences or have lost touch with them, and yet they uncannily share family memories, habits, and patterns of thought. Although Frances Wingate and Janet Bird are at first glance vastly different—the former self-confident, independent, and careless; the latter timid, housebound, and excessively cautious—the narrator suggests that Frances is merely a more highly evolved version of her provincial young cousin. When the two get to know each other, after an initial distrust and antipathy, they discover that they share a kind of intelligence and wit. Janet is what Frances would be had her father not gone to university and left Tockley; Frances is what Janet has the potential to be if she were to get away from her brutish husband and enlarge her experience.

Structurally, the novel moves away from isolated narratives about the various separated family members toward a uniting of these relatives into a shared experience and the same principal narrative. Frances eventually meets Janet and another cousin, David Ollerenshaw, of whom, due to an old family breach, she had not known, and these three rekindle the ties among the various branches of the Ollerenshaw family. Thus, subconscious family bonds become conscious as Frances and her cousins come to appreciate and cultivate them.

Although most of Drabble's novels ultimately affirm family ties, many of the protagonists initially attempt to deny or sever their connection with their families. As young people struggling to discover their own identities, they need to understand "where [they] began and the family ended" (*Realms*, p. 97). And so they usually leave home as soon as they can, for university or London or marriage, and try to carve out a life different from their parents'. Many of them try to escape their heritage by marrying someone of a different background or life-style. Often the spouse's motive is the same. Thus, Emma, with her refined, academic family background, marries David Evans, a flashy, lower-class Welshman. The two hope that in creating this "curious conjunction" (*Garrick Year*, p. 26) they have "committed [themselves] to unfamiliarity, so that [they] would be forever voluntarily exiled, with no pernicious hope of retreat, from that lush Cambridge garden and that sour four-roomed cottage in North Wales" (*Garrick Year*, p. 32). Again, Jane, an aspiring poet rebelling against her bourgeois, provincial parents, marries Malcolm Gray, a musician rebelling against his lower-class background. Both believe they have thereby become "exiled from their past, united by their isolation, by their artistic efforts, by their lack of identity with their own history" (*Waterfall*, p. 109). In *The Needle's Eye* thrifty, hard-working Simon marries materialistic Julie Phillips because he is attracted to her vulgar *nouveau riche* background—the very antithesis of his puritanical, working-class one; and wealthy, aristocratic Rose cuts herself off from her family by marrying an impoverished Greek. A final example is *The Middle Ground*'s protagonist, Kate, who as a young woman married Stuart Armstrong because she found his unconventional, bohemian family so appealing in contrast to her own stultifying working-class one.

However, Drabble believes that one's identity is in good part constituted by inherited family traits and early childhood environment. Therefore, a fuller understanding of oneself results from a recognition of these factors. And so, many of her characters eventually feel moved to investigate their roots. Drabble uses a particular plot device in certain novels to demonstrate the protagonist's growing awareness of the significance of her heritage: an episode toward the end of the novel in which the protagonist pays a visit to her family home and embarks upon a profoundly affecting psychological journey into the past, either her own childhood or the family past.

These journeys all begin with the protagonist's poking through old cupboards and drawers, in pursuit of an elusive key to her past. The significance of this activity is illuminated by Gaston Bachelard in his chapter entitled "Drawers, Chests, and Wardrobes" in *The Poetics of Space*. He points out, "Wardrobes with their shelves, desks with their drawers, and chests with their false bottoms are veritable organs of the secret psychological life."[3] Delving into them, therefore, is the protagonists' first step in their quest for their past. They all emerge from this journey with greater psychological integration. This pattern occurs in *Jerusalem the Golden, The Realms of Gold,* and *The Needle's Eye*.

Of all Drabble's protagonists, Clara Maugham is the most intent upon severing herself from her family. Yet even she senses that it is psychologically soothing to be a part of a family network and destiny; indeed, although she has left her own family, she has latched onto a surrogate one, the Denhams. However, try as she does to regard them as her "family by proxy" (*Jerusalem*, p. 200), she is haunted by the feeling that her connection with them is a forced bond, whereas the "ties of blood" (*Jerusalem*, p. 200) are inevitable and tenacious. Clara feels that she has "gained somewhere in her total severance," but she is "at the same time uneasily aware that there is no such thing as severance, that connections endure till death, that blood is after all blood" (*Jerusalem*, p. 153). Trying to deny these connections requires continuous effort and exercise of the will. Suddenly struck by how exhausting and risky it is to live in this manner, she wonders in desperation, "What will happen to me, what will happen if I should ever lose my nerve?" (*Jerusalem*, p. 193).

Clara, then, is in a difficult psychological situation, both desirous of the kind of strong family connection and identity the Denham children have and yet despising her own family. This conflict is eventually mitigated, however, toward the end of the novel when she is summoned from London back to her hometown because her widowed mother is dying in the hospital. Spending the night alone in her old home, she is mysteriously drawn to her mother's bedroom and finds herself going through all the cupboards and drawers, "searching, looking anxiously for she knew not what, for some small white powdery bones, for some ghost of departed life" (*Jerusalem*, p. 227). Subconsciously, she is looking for something that will confirm her connection with her mother. She finds this in the form of old photographs, poems, and diaries, which reveal, to Clara's amazement, that as a young girl her mother had been strikingly similar to herself, embracing the same hopes and dreams. Clara is deeply saddened to realize that life's disappointments and realities have deformed her mother's girlhood spirit; yet at the same time she feels "a sense of shocked relief, for she was glad that she had however miserably pre-existed, she felt, for the first time, the satisfaction of her true descent" (*Jerusalem*, p. 228). Although nothing in her external situation has changed and there is every indication she will return to her aimless, rootless existence in London, she has at least found temporary psychological solace in being reminded of her roots.

Frances Wingate is more permanently affected by her return to her family home. She is considerably older than Clara and more consciously aware of the human need to feel part of a family chain. In quest of this elusive goal she makes a trip back to Tockley, the provincial northern town of her ancestors, the Ollerenshaws, where she spent childhood summers at her grandparents' rural cottage. This journey is a prelude to a later, more significant one in which she visits her late great-aunt's cottage and goes through a psychological experience similar to Clara's. She spends the evening alone in the house and looks through drawers and cupboards with a vague sense of searching for some clue to the past. She finds old family photographs, papers, and other "records going back into the dim reaches of the dusty Ollerenshaw past" (*Realms*, p. 229).

Frances' quest, however, is more conscious and intellectual than Clara's because, being an archaeologist, Frances believes that one can better understand the present and one's own life by understanding the past and one's ancestors. She therefore conducts her search through the Ollerenshaw records in an archaeological spirit, likening the old letters, coins, medals, and other objects to archaeological artifacts, observing that they are "nearly as indecipherable as hieroglyphics, nearly as sparse in their information as Phoenician shopping lists" (*Realms*, p. 299). Although she notes that it is a "worthless collection" in comparison to many of her archaeological finds, such as "the prosperous relics of Tizouk" (*Realms*, p. 299), it is personally valuable in that it enables her to discover her heritage. In perusing the documents she begins to sense her place in the family chain. Like her ancestors, who worked hard to raise themselves from agricultural laborers to successful shopkeepers and shoemakers, she too has been propelled by ambition.

Her sense of family identity deepens when, like Clara, she discovers in a female ancestor's life a parallel to her own. A packet of old letters reveals that her great-aunt Con in her youth had been in love with a married man, who, although he loved her in return, could not bring himself to leave his wife. Frances is herself involved in this kind of relationship and so she reads the letters with increasing fascination, speculating about her aunt's life. As she does so, she begins to feel "curiously at home, and private, feeding twigs into her own hearth. Perhaps she herself would live here, taking over where Con had left off" (*Realms*, p. 303). Significantly, when a passerby comes up to the door, having noticed the light from the fire, he tells Frances that she gave him a fright, explaining, "You could have been Constance herself, fifty years younger. In this light" (*Realms*, p. 304). The experience of identifying with her ancestors has filled such a psychological need in Frances that she attempts to perpetuate it by moving her family to Tockley and buying her great-aunt's cottage.

The ending of the novel telescopes the future, giving glimpses of Frances' life over the next several years and revealing that she does indeed maintain greater contact with her extended family.

The third novel in which Drabble uses this type of quest pattern is *The Needle's Eye*. Like Clara, Rose has put all her efforts into forging a life that is the antithesis of her parents'. However, Rose's goal is more laudable: whereas Clara is in search of excitement and intrigue, Rose is trying to build her life around the Christian ideals of charity, humility, and modesty by giving away her inherited wealth and dwelling in a shabby neighborhood. Another difference lies in their respective attitudes toward their parents. Rose does not fear, as does Clara, that if she relaxes her will she may snap back into the family mold; on the contrary, she suspects that it was a freak accident for her to have been born of such parents, with whom she feels no connection. Instead of comforting her, however, this notion has always disturbed her; she would rather feel herself to be a link in a family chain, no matter how unattractive the other members, than completely isolated and exiled. In vain has she tried to trace a

> natural connection between herself and her parentage, discovering in herself her mother's hypochondria with every sore throat, her father's inhumanity with her own preference for the total as opposed to the individual. I, like him, she would say to herself, am stubborn beyond belief, I too am partisan, it is simply that accident has forced me to take the other part.
>
> But she did not believe these reasonings. Transcendence loomed over her head like a great owl. (*Needle's Eye*, p. 316)

Toward the end of the novel, a series of events causes Rose to end up at her parents' home one weekend, after several years away. The situation of finding herself once again in the setting and atmosphere of her childhood triggers her desire to understand why she is so different from her parents. Simon Camish, who has accompanied her, is similarly affected, wondering to himself at dinner that evening, "Where had she come from, how had it happened? People do not grow out of nothing, they do not spring from the earth. Somewhere in this house, in these two disagreeable ageing people, in this dingy dining-room, lay the grounds for her fantastic notions. He felt almost as though there must be some spirit, some clue, hovering in the air around them" (*Needle's Eye*, pp. 311–12).

It is this clue to her own character development that Rose suddenly feels compelled to discover. Later that evening, she bids the others good-night and retires, haunted by a "sense of some appointment more significant than confession, which awaited her upstairs" (*Needle's Eye*, p. 323). Like Clara and Frances, she is mysteriously moved to look for "relics of the past, in the bottom of a cupboard or a wardrobe, in a broom closet, in a tea chest or a suitcase or an old box" (*Needle's Eye*, p. 316). Her quest directs her to the bedroom formerly inhabited by her governess, Noreen. The atmosphere of this room, peculiarly powerful to her as a child, floods Rose with intense memories, causing her to relive several crucial formative episodes of her childhood. Although this experience does not result in her discovering similarities between herself and her parents, it does provide her with a greater sense of psychological integration. Her memories enable her to grasp the way in which the major ingredients of her childhood—her cold, aloof, wealthy parents and her obsessively religious, superstitious governess—combined to influence her personality development, and so she no longer feels that her character is a freak accident. Like Clara and Frances, she can now move on in her life with a firmer grasp of her identity and a sense of wholeness.

A variation of this quest pattern appears in *The Middle Ground*. Like many of the other protagonists, Kate as a girl strove to break from the family mold, and to a large extent she succeeded in that she escaped the neurosis which should have been her inheritance given her agoraphobic mother and paranoid father. The boisterous lifestyle and attitude she subsequently adopted has sustained her through young adulthood; but with middle age arrives a feeling of emptiness which stirs in Kate the desire to reconnect with her family and her past.

Like the other women, she journeys back to her childhood haunts, with a vague, almost mystical sense of mission. Winding her way along the sewage embankment she had walked so often as a girl, she feels that she is travelling backwards in time and that she is on the verge of profound insights into her own psychology: "Her heart beat uncomfortably fast as she walked over the first of these [iron manhole] covers; recollections just beyond the reach of memory gathered in the distance, took shape as she approached" (*Middle Ground*, p. 112). Leaning down and sniffing the sewer smells through the grille, as she had frequently done of old, she feels "slightly weak with shame and excitement. Was this what she had come for, was this the window, the grille through which she should escape the prison of the present into the past, where the dark spirits swam in the fast-moving flood?" (*Middle Ground*, p. 117).

As was mentioned in chapter 3, the "dark tunnels, the mysterious network" (*Middle Ground*, p. 117) of the sewer system become for Kate an image of her own psyche, with its intricate, interlocking paths reaching back into childhood. She launches into a protracted series of reminiscences, which reveal her ineradicable tie with her childhood self and her family: "She'd thought she had moved and changed, but she hadn't. She'd been offered flight, escape, transformation, but for some reason she'd managed to impose herself, her old self, even on the Armstrongs" (*Middle Ground*, p. 114). Furthermore, she finds comfort in this connection and begins to wonder whether it is psychologically damaging to tear up one's roots: "This is my country, thought Kate. Tatty, low, obdurate. Was it wrong, perhaps, to move?" (*Middle Ground*, p. 114). In thus accepting her heritage, Kate moves toward psychological reintegration. Her feelings of isolation and disconnectedness fade, and by the end of the novel she has regained her psychological footing.

In addition to the journey-into-the-past motif, another way Drabble demonstrates the individual's deep psychological attachment to the family web is her display of the tenacious bonds siblings often share. This involvement can be a positive factor in a person'a life, as it is for Frances Wingate, who as a young girl developed a special relationship with her older brother, Hugh. They established an intimate pattern of talking late into the night about the subjects that deeply concerned them. Although as an adult Frances rarely sees Hugh, when she does they revert to the intimate, confidential rapport they developed as children. In middle age, visiting one weekend with her children at Hugh's family's cottage, she waits until all the others have gone to bed to sit up with him and discuss the fears that have recently been obsessing her.

Sometimes, however, a sibling relationship has pernicious effects throughout a person's life and is responsible for certain psychological problems or personality disorders. Alison Murray, though well into middle age, has not been able to shed her childhood guilt regarding her older sister. When they were children Rosemary developed an intense jealousy of Alison because of the latter's superior looks and popularity. Although as adults they are not close and rarely see each other, when Alison learns of Rosemary's mastectomy she is gripped for months with guilt and terror. Like a child, she superstitiously fears the same thing will happen to her, that she will be "punished" because she "gave Rosemary cancer of the breast" (*Ice Age*, p. 97). Her adult mind, of course, knows that this is nonsense; nonetheless, her childhood guilt is so ingrained that she cannot shake her irrational feelings.

Sibling jealousy also profoundly influences the personality development of Alison's older daughter. When the younger daughter, Molly, was born with cerebral palsy, Alison was intensely aware of the potential inferiority complex the child could develop by comparing herself to her healthy, good-looking older sister, Jane. She therefore insisted that the latter be kind and loving toward Molly. But her plan backfires—ironically, Jane is the one to be consumed with jealousy and resentment, because of her mother's preoccupation with Molly. It suddenly strikes Alison, when Jane is eighteen, that the girl's bitter, selfish personality is largely the result of this difficult sibling situation. Undoubtedly, Jane will be hampered for the rest of her life by this irrational resentment, just as Alison is psychologically handicapped by her guilt toward Rosemary.

Although Kate Armstrong and her older brother, Peter, were very close and loyal to one another as children, as they grew up they grew apart, Kate becoming socially successful and Peter turning increasingly odd and nervous. As adults they move in very different circles, rarely meet, and are critical of one another's life-styles. And yet they are psychologically bound up with one another in an intense way. Peter is apparently insanely jealous of Kate, for he sends her anonymous hate mail, and Kate suspects that her success was somehow the cause of his failure. She spends a great deal of time and anxiety analyzing the influence she and Peter had on each other's personality development. "There was no denying it," she observes, "the idea of Peter was inextricably linked in her mind with whatever it was that had gone wrong with her own life. He'd occupied much less of her conscious life than Stuart, Hunt, Evelyn, Ted, Hugo, yet there he was, standing in her mind like a dam in a river" (*Middle Ground*, p. 125).

Another difficult, involved sibling relationship is portrayed in *A Summer Bird-Cage*. Although Sarah expresses disapproval and dislike of her cold, glamorous older sister, Louise, she is irresistibly drawn to her. This is revealed by her spending almost as much time in the narrative discussing and analyzing Louise and Louise's life as she does on herself and her own. Narrative flashbacks reveal the source of her ambivalent, complex attitude: as a child she craved Louise's attention and affection but was continually rebuffed.

Though now buried under layers of defense and rationalization, this unsatisfied need has become a part of her psychology. For example, her conviction that her own life is drab is no doubt the result of having grown up in the shadow of mysterious, notorious Louise. In the early part of her narrative, Sarah rashly tries to dismiss her sibling connection by telling herself that Louise is "merely and accidentally [her] sister" (*Bird-Cage*, p. 80); but ultimately she comes to terms with her attachment. During the course of the novel, because Louise makes some disastrous errors and thereby shows herself to be an ordinary human being, Sarah learns to view her objectively. This results in her realizing that although she dislikes much about Louise, there is a deep, instinctive bond between them, for "blood is thicker than water" (*Bird-Cage*, p. 208).

Drabble's most elaborate display of sibling involvement occurs in *The Waterfall*. Here, however, the bond exists not between two actual sisters but between two cousins who are like sisters, Jane Gray and Lucy Otford. As Jane says, Lucy is "my sister: more nearly my sister than my own sister was" (*Waterfall*, p. 135). Whereas Sarah attempts to deny for a time her sibling attachment, Jane, mystically and superstitiously inclined, embraces the notion that she and Lucy are destined to be alter-egos, claiming that her cousin is her "fate, [her] example: her effect upon me was incalculable" (*Waterfall*, p. 136). The two girls, only a fortnight apart in age and the daughters of two very close sisters, are uncannily similar in temperament. They instinctively understand and respect each other's need for reticence and privacy and when together converse in a cryptic, almost telegraphic fashion, so intuitive is each one's grasp of the other's meaning. The alter-ego theme becomes increasingly pronounced as Jane proceeds to fall in love with Lucy's husband, carry on a prolonged affair with him, and go off on a secret trip with him in which she travels as "Mrs. Lucy Otford." Although Lucy is momentarily angry when she discovers their treachery, she so much identifies with Jane that she rapidly adapts to the situation. The novel's ending indicates that the two cousins, neither of whom puts much stock in marital fidelity, may very well share James for the rest of their lives.

In an interview Drabble explained that her relationship with her older sister, the novelist A. S. Byatt, has been one of the crucial formative factors in her psychological development. Although having harbored since childhood a certain amount of jealousy and resentment toward this sister, she at the same time feels a deep bond with her, noting that they are very similar and that their lives have been parallel in many ways.[4] Interestingly, her sister's first novel, *The Game* (1967), is an intensive study of a difficult, intricate relationship between two sisters from youth into middle age. A childhood pattern of relating to one another, consisting of jealousy and coldness on the part of the older sister, Cassandra, and obsequiousness and insecurity on the part of the younger, Julia, becomes so ingrained that they continue to act it out, though more indirectly, in adulthood. In fact, Cassandra's jealousy so distorts her mind that it contributes to her eventual suicide.[5]

Drabble's view of sibling involvement is never as dark as that expressed by her sister in *The Game*. Although she recognizes that family relationships sometimes handicap people, she usually depicts the family in a positive light. Indeed, some of her most memorable scenes portray the happy confusion of family life, and some of her most appealing characters are those who thrive in this atmosphere: Rose, Emily, and Christopher of *The Needle's Eye*, Frances of *The Realms of Gold*, Babs of *The Ice Age*, and Kate of *The Middle Ground*. But the family serves an even more important function than simply providing happiness for its members; it is a haven against life's chaos and destruction. Belonging to a family is a way of being connected with the eternal, and there is something comforting and fortifying about viewing oneself as a part of a larger whole rather than as a discrete individual. An underlying structure in Drabble's novels is the protagonist's movement away from an isolated, existential orientation and into the bosom of family.[6]

A Summer Bird-Cage ends with the two sisters engaging in a lengthy, intimate tête-à-tête, after having been emotionally estranged for most of their lives. There is a warm, upbeat quality to this scene, as the two girls sit in front of the fire sipping cocoa and talking late into the night. This is a foreshadowing of the endings of later Drabble novels, which often involve a life-affirming family reunion scene.

The Garrick Year concludes in such a manner. Throughout the novel Emma has been struggling with feelings of alienation from her husband and marriage and with the desire to establish her own identity. However, toward the end she gradually loses interest in these struggles and submerges her identity in the role of mother and protector. Although still less than content with her marriage, she comes to accept it by regarding it archetypally, adopting Hume's view of the function of marriage: " 'Whoever considers,' Hume says, 'the length and feebleness of human infancy, with the concern which both sexes naturally have for their offspring, will easily perceive that there must be a union of male and female for the education of the young, and that this union must be of considerable duration' " (*Garrick Year*, p. 220).

As the final scene reveals, Emma and David are indeed happiest when most fully involved in their roles of mother and father, delighting in and protecting their young. The novel concludes with the family going on an idyllic outing in the country; Emma observes, "Had David and I been two entirely different people we might well that afternoon have been entirely happy: and even being what we were, we did not do too badly" (*Garrick Year*, p. 221). Drabble symbolically suggests that the family is a haven against the evil and destruction of life by having this happy scene take place in the midst of dangers: as they leave the meadow Emma notices a poisonous snake clutching at a sheep's belly. Alarmed but philosophical about the situation, she reflects, "But 'Oh well, so what', is all that one can say, the Garden of Eden was crawling with them too, and David and I managed to lie amongst them for one whole pleasant afternoon. One just has to keep on and to pretend, for the sake of the children, not to notice. Otherwise one might just as well stay at home" (*Garrick Year*, p. 221). The family, then, can be a comforting, nurturing institution, a spot of safety and stability in the midst of uncertainty.

In *The Needle's Eye* Rose goes through a movement similar to Emma's, from being preoccupied with herself as an individual to foregoing this concern and devoting herself to the needs of the family. Although she is reluctant to resume traditional family life and feels bitter once she has done so, nonetheless she is susceptible to its attractions. Otherwise, she would not have succumbed to her former husband's pressure to take him back. It is on a family outing, with something of the quality of Emma's, that she begins to be inexorably pulled back into family life. She, her former husband, their three children, and their friend Simon hike to a remote beach for a picnic and an afternoon of swimming and gathering cockles. Drabble is always attracted to this type of scene—a messy human jumble of children and parents—and describes it in an appealing way. Although Rose and Christopher bicker and Rose occasionally snaps at the children, an atmosphere of warmth and safety pervades the episode. The havenlike nature of the situation is underscored by the fact that it takes place in the midst of evils and dangers: the police are looking for Christopher to serve an injunction against him for threatening to kidnap his children; thoughts of death are thrust upon the group when Rose mentions once having found a corpse in a ditch they pass; and the omniscient narrator informs us that while they are laughing and enjoying themselves, a few miles away on a deserted beach a yacht is landing a group of frightened illegal immigrants. Thus, this secure family gathering is surrounded by reminders of the harsh real world.

A similar scene takes place in *The Realms of Gold*, when members of Frances' family gather at Hugh Ollerenshaw's country cottage. There is the same cozy, safe atmosphere and the same feeling of temporarily shutting out life's evils. For Frances, it is an escape from the feelings of anxiety and alienation that usually obsess her: "She liked being in a room full of her own family, she felt safe with Natasha sitting there reading, with Daisy with the baby on her knee, with Hugh drunk and talkative, with Stephen limp and pleasant and intelligent. The light flickered from the fire, and glinted from the mirror on the wall, from the glasses, the gold rims of the coffee cups. . . . It felt safe, it felt like the country, undisturbed, with the black night and no lights in it outside the small windowpanes, timeless. It was an old cottage, it felt old and safe like a secure infancy" (*Realms*, p. 186).

In *The Ice Age* Drabble again emphasizes the safety of the family group. Warm, maternal Kitty Friedmann is the hub of her large extended family; her comfortable home is usually filled with relatives. It storms the night Alison Murray, a distant relative, spends at her house, and the contrast between the destruction and chaos outside and the warmth and security inside underscores the important function of the family. Lying in her bed, listening to the wind and looking at her rose-patterned wallpaper and thick carpet, Kitty reflects, "In here, it was warm, and safe, and comfortable" (*Ice Age*, p. 161). A conscious optimist, she is aware of the need to cultivate this warmth and safety, to banish from one's thoughts the evils of life. She therefore will not let herself think about Max, her late husband, who was gruesomely killed, just as she pushes off thoughts of "the six million Jews, and those who died in the Soviet labor camps, and those who were languishing now in camps and prisons. The black wastes, where the winds of hell perpetually howled" (*Ice Age*, p. 161). Instead, she strives heroically to build up a fortress for her family: "The house was solid and quiet. The walls were thick. Outside, the wind blew, and for a moment, before she fell asleep, Kitty imagined that the spirit of Max was pouring in the gale and streaming against her outer windows, beseeching entrance. But the house was well insulated, and she would not, could not admit him. If she admitted him, she could not survive, and she had to survive. For the children, the grandchildren" (*Ice Age*, p. 162).

That same night Alison, lying in another bedroom in Kitty's house, observes that the "family is a good, multiple, reparable fortification against death: when one member dies, the gap is filled by another. A communal survival" (*Ice Age*, p. 160). Although her childhood family was weak and her married family life ended in divorce, she longs for a strong family network like Kitty's. She and Anthony Keating are trying to create such a situation: they have bought a house in the country and are planning to marry and retire there, with their various children coming for weekends. In *The Realms of Gold* Frances Wingate and Karel Schmidt are inclined to a similar idyllic goal: the novel ends with their marrying and retiring to Frances' country cottage with their respective children. The establishment of their family is cemented when Frances' daughter and Karel's son marry and produce a child.

Finally, Kate Armstrong is another protagonist who resolves her existential despair in part by immersing herself in family. However, in *The Middle Ground* "family" takes on a much broader meaning than in the other novels. Because a major reason for Kate's psychological dislocation is that her children are growing up and will soon no longer need her, she finds herself developing a new kind of family structure, one which includes the various friends — old and new, English and foreign — who gravitate toward her and her warm, vibrant home. Although she has at times felt oppressed by the intrusion of these people, toward the end of the novel she is suddenly flooded with happiness when she realizes that they have in fact become her "family."

The book ends with a party, the classic comic device described by Northrop Frye in which the various members of family and community are harmoniously brought together in some sort of celebration.[7] This particular celebration is a combination birthday party for Kate's son Mark, just home from his first term at university, welcome-home party for Evelyn, recently released from the hospital, and going-away party for Hugo, about to set off for Bagdad, and Mujid, the Iraqui student who has been staying at Kate's and is soon to return home. But the underlying and most significant purpose of the party is to celebrate life, and Kate's renewed interest in it after her long period of despair. Sitting in the midst of friends and children a few hours before the festivity is to begin, Kate experi-

ences an epiphany-like insight—very Woolfian in quality—into the
importance of family and community:

> How could she ever have found [Mujid] so irritating? Could
> you get to like anyone, given the time? Not that she wasn't
> glad to get rid of him, enough is enough, but nevertheless,
> how good that it should end so well, and even as she was
> thinking this, looking around her family circle, feeling as she
> sat there a sense of immense calm, strength, centrality, as
> though she were indeed the centre of a circle, in the most
> old-fashioned of ways, a moving circle—oh, there is no lan-
> guage left to describe such things, we have called it all so much
> in question, but imagine a circle even so, a circle and a moving
> sphere, for this is her house and there she sits, she has every-
> thing and nothing, I give her everything and nothing—even
> as she sat, the phone went, and it was Beatrice Mourre from
> Paris [the mother of Mujid's Lebanese fiancée, Simone, and
> an old friend of Kate's], wanting to thank Kate, wanting to
> wish Mark a happy birthday, screeching excitedly, a voice not
> heard in nineteen years, "Ah, my dear, I remember you as
> though it were *yesterday*"—and Kate shouted back, unneces-
> sarily loud across the many miles of land and sea, that it had
> been her joy, her pleasure, to have been able to look after
> Mujid and Simone: and as soon as she put the phone down, it
> went again, this time for Ruth [Kate's daughter], then again,
> and the lull was over, and the circle broke up into its various
> spheres of activity. (*Middle Ground*, p. 275)

In addition to community, Drabble creates yet another dimension
to Kate's family: she draws into it characters who have appeared in
her other novels. Kate has invited to the party Gabriel Denham, a
producer friend and the father of one of Kate's son's friends, along
with his former wife, Phillipa. The reader will remember these
characters from *Jerusalem the Golden*. Also included is Rosamund
Stacey, the Stennetts' intellectual neighbor and, of course, the protagonist of *The Millstone*. Although this device may have been just
playful whimsy on the author's part, its effect is to enhance the
theme of Kate's pervasive family network. Furthermore, it suggests
that Margaret Drabble has begun to view her novels as constituting
an extended fictional community of people.

Drabble's protagonists, then, gravitate toward the family, although the families they establish are often unconventional. The

author is implying that although society is changing and divorce is rampant, certain primeval needs remain. She expresses this view through the observations of Sarah Bennett, who reflects on her older sister's unconventional marriage as she accompanies Louise to meet the latter's lover at the theatre:

> So Covent Garden and Drury Lane go on, next door to each other, and though the details change, the way of life is the same. I realized, as we walked there, that what Louise was doing was a reversal of roles: she was taking the man's part, calling at the theatre instead of being called for. She was in the tradition, but she had reversed it, instead of opting out completely, as most girls are now obliged to do. I felt a glow of admiration: she was, after all, striking a blow for civilization in her behaviour, not, as it first had seemed, for anarchy. Why that should be admirable I didn't go into, but I was sure it was: it was braver than to abandon the game completely. To force marriage into a mold of one's own, while still preserving the name of marriage — it seemed an enterprise worth consideration. Indeed, there was almost something classic in her position, something more deeply rooted in the shapes of life than the eternal triangle of a woman's magazine. (*Bird-Cage*, p. 195)[8]

She concludes that Louise is "part of an unbroken line, rather than a freak" (*Bird-Cage*, p. 195).

Thus, Drabble's novels affirm the importance of family, and the plots often involve an eventual reunion of estranged family members. While this device is a long-standing convention of comic plots, Drabble does not merely rely on it as a handy way to conclude a novel. Rather, this structure reflects her particular views about the individual's relationship to the world. The protagonists discover that although their characters are unique, to a certain extent they derive from inherited family traits and tendencies. Accepting this fact provides one with greater psychological integration. Furthermore, it is comforting to be a part of a family, which buffers one from some of life's inevitable harshness. This insight is voiced by Jane Gray, after she has struggled through several months of isolation and existential anxiety: "Throw away choice, emancipation, distinction, selection, friendship: in favour of enforced, compulsive, abrasive family ties. Organic ties" (*Waterfall*, p. 112).

However, in having her characters become less concerned with themselves as individuals and more involved in their family roles, Drabble is not suggesting that they are squelching their own identities. Instead, she feels that this move signals the onset of maturity. In her published response to Monica Manheimer's article, "The Search for Identity in *The Needle's Eye*," she explains her view: "I have just read, for the first time, an account of Erikson's theory of the eight ages of man. It seems to me that to stop short at self-realisation, and the achieving of one's own identity, is to refuse to move into the eighth stage, in which (if I have got it right) one assumes responsibility for one's community and one's succeeding generations. Rose and Simon try to move into the eighth stage. *The Realms of Gold* characters do also, but they are allowed a greater degree of self-realisation as an accidental bit of luck, as a by-product."[9]

Drabble herself, if her body of fiction is to be taken as a reflection of her own growth, has moved in this direction. Whereas her first protagonist is a husbandless, childless young woman unable to commit herself to marriage and engrossed in exclusively personal concerns, later protagonists are embedded in increasingly broader family structures. The women of her middle novels are involved in only their nuclear families, but her most recent protagonists embrace much wider family groups: their ancestors, their extended families, the families of second spouses, and their community of friends. An important development in Drabble's fiction, then, is a movement away from self-centered individualism toward greater social responsibility.

5

Imagination: The Role of Vision

The dark, sometimes menacing quality of Drabble's fictional universe is mitigated not only by the soothing powers of nature and family but also by the human imagination and spirit. The protagonists' capacity for humor and joy was discussed in chapter 2. In addition, they all possess a certain visionary tendency which enables them to endure the dreariness or difficulty of their lives—an intuition of or belief in a more significant order of reality than that to which they are accustomed. Some of them merely suspect the existence of this other order; others catch glimpses or signs of it; and still others manage to attain it for a period of time. But even if they never realize their vision, and most of them do not, they are cheered and sustained by these intuitions and glimpses.

The visionary reality assumes a variety of forms, but these can be broadly classified as the spiritual and the secular. The spiritual vision ranges from a traditional notion of heaven and God, which Rose Vassiliou and Anthony Keating hold, to a generalized sense of a metaphysical force informing and directing human life. Most Drabble protagonists possess the latter sense, as is evident by their tendency to suspect the hand of fate or providence in apparently random events. Although, as has been shown in chapter 2, the characters often perceive this metaphysical force as malicious, some of them at times take a more hopeful view, believing that there is an ultimate reason for life's misfortune and chaos. They suspect that if allowed a glimpse of the divine plan, they would see that it is benevolent. Drabble has said that she herself possesses a strong need to "perceive this pattern" and that she has a "deep conviction that if you were to get high up enough over the world, you would see things that look like coincidence are, in fact, part of a pattern."[1] Furthermore, she has a "deep faith that it will all be revealed to [her] one day.

One day [she] shall just see into the heart of the whole thing."[2]

Many of her protagonists share this faith and have moments when they feel on the brink of revelation. Jane Gray, for example, senses that divine insight is imminent when she is in a near-fatal automobile accident. When the revelation ultimately eludes her, however, she feels sorely disappointed:

> I thought that death had visited me in person, as an angel, as a presence, and had denied me the final vision, the final revelation. Knowledge hung so near me then, and had not yielded itself up to me: I have always cherished the faith that at the moment of death I would be immeasurably illumined, that the mystery would be made clear to my astonished gaze, and I sat there cheated, betrayed, done out of wisdom. The quality of one's living will determine the quality of one's dying, and I said to myself as I crouched there trembling that I had had faith, I had believed in the significance of life and that God had no right to deny me the white lights that I had hoped for. (*Waterfall*, p. 224)

But then she regains her faith by reflecting, "God had hidden his face for some later unveiling, perhaps" (*Waterfall*, p. 224).

Whereas Jane believes that revelation is contained in the moment of death, Frances Wingate suspects that it is at the heart of her psychological depressions, sensing that her "illness [has] some deep spiritual significance" (*Realms*, p. 97). However, her depression always passes without the secret's being revealed, and she, like Jane, is left feeling "obscurely cheated, as though she had missed something of final importance by not concentrating hard enough. This was the worst thing of all, the sense of loss. As though one waited, constantly, for something that never happened, was never revealed" (*Realms*, p. 8).

For Rosamund Stacey, the condition of pregnancy brings her into contact with the metaphysical order of reality. As Frances regards her illness as a portent from God, so Rosamund suspects that her pregnancy is a sign of "a different, non-rational order of things" (*Millstone*, p. 74). But like the other women, although she feels on the verge of seeing into this order, she never does so: "it was as though I were waiting for some link to be revealed to me that would make sense of disconnections, though I had no evidence at all that it existed. At times I had a vague and complicated sense that this pregnancy had been sent to me in order to reveal to me a scheme of things totally different from the scheme which I inhabited" (*Millstone*, p. 75).

Rose Vassiliou's and Anthony Keating's spiritual visions are more specifically Christian. As a small child Rose was inculcated with religious attitudes by her Bible-preaching governess and was particularly affected by Christ's warning that "it is easier for a camel to go through the eye of a needle than for a rich man to enter the kingdom of God." Since her parents were extremely wealthy as well as cold and aloof, these words helped develop in the impressionable child a vision of a Christian life of poverty and humility that would embody the grace and beauty her family's life lacked. She has carried this ideal into adulthood, attempting to achieve it by renouncing her wealth and living in a humble fashion.

In contrast to Rose, Anthony Keating develops his interest in spiritual matters later in life, after years of having been concerned exclusively with the material. But as with Rose, his embracing of God and Christian theology springs from a need to cope with unhappy circumstances. He has experienced a series of worldly reversals, when he is suddenly struck by a thought that plants in him the seeds of his religious birth: "I do not know how man can do without God" (*Ice Age*, p. 265). His initial attraction to this question derives from intellectual curiosity rather than faith; he is not yet ready "to ask for a revelation from his creator" (*Ice Age*, p. 265). However, when the worst of his reversals comes—imprisonment in a communist country—he begins to turn his thoughts increasingly to God and spiritual matters. Deeply influenced by *The Consolation of Philosophy*, he decides to write his own book "about the nature of God and the possibility of religious faith" (*Ice Age*, p. 293). Like Boethius, he comes to believe that God has an ultimately benevolent reason for making human beings suffer, suspecting that his own difficulties have been sent as a trial of his faith: "If God did not appoint this trial for me, then how could it be that I should be asked to endure it, he asks. He cannot bring himself to believe in the random malice of the fates, those three gray sisters. He is determined, alone, to justify the ways of God to man" (*Ice Age*, p. 294).

Anthony develops the same propensity for seeking out revelations that characterizes other Drabble protagonists. Just as Jane, Frances, and Rosamund regard certain situations as signs or glimpses of metaphysical reality and believe that if they concentrate they will experience the revelation contained therein, so Anthony "cannot evade the idea that God has given him the chance to work out the first causes and the last causes, and that he must not reject it. Those long winter days alone at High Rook House [his country home in northern England] were a warning and a preparation. He should have concentrated harder then, but was too distracted by the memories of the living, by the immediate future" (*Ice Age*, p. 294). Now that he dwells in closer contact with the spiritual realm, he is more open to divine signs and portents. On the last page of the novel, spotting a rare, beautiful bird while working in the prison yard, he is filled with joy, taking it to be a "messenger from God, an angel, a promise" (*Ice Age*, p. 295).

The spiritual vision, then, is for some Drabble protagonists a vague intuition of a metaphysical power operating in the world and for others a more traditional Christian faith in God. But in both cases the vision has the same effect upon the individual: it enables him or her to endure an otherwise dreary or difficult life by suggesting that there is a more significant order of reality beyond the immediate, phenomenal one.

The secular vision, which accomplishes a similar effect, plays a crucial role in the psychologies of nearly all the protagonists. Drabble's abiding interest in this psychological syndrome is suggested by the fact that it constitutes the focal point of many of her short stories and is a major driving force in most of the protagonists' lives. The characteristics of the secular vision are as follows: it involves the desire for a life charged with a beauty, richness, and intensity—of an emotional, social, moral, or intellectual nature—not found in the protagonists' customary reality; the protagonists strive to achieve this heightened reality but ultimately most of them acknowledge that it lies only in the realm of the imagination, not in the phenomenal world; glimpses of and brief experiences with the visionary reality are fraught with mystery and significance; and the envisioned existence resembles either a work of art of a mythic golden world, some visions combining aspects of both.

Although not until *Jerusalem the Golden* does the pursuit of vision become a major concern in Drabble's novels, this theme is adumbrated in earlier works. Sarah Bennett's and Emma Evans' obsession with the thinness of their own lives and their desire for more intense, adventurous ones prefigures the later protagonists' attachments to visions. And the two women's attraction to the unfamiliar and mysterious will be shared by later protagonists, whose visions are essentially elusive. Sarah, for example, prefers brief, temporary encounters with strange men at parties to familiar, established relationships, because of the air of mystery and infinite possibility the former possess. She explains, "I don't know what I am missing in my life of permanent and valuable contact, though I feel its absence, but at least from time to time I get something that I would never get were I not so displaced—the sudden confidence, the momentary illumination of feeling, ships passing and moreover signalling in the dark" (*Bird-Cage*, p. 108).

Emma too is susceptible to situations that are faught with suggestion and never-tested possibility; for example, she is haunted by images of "that somebody like myself that I see once a year in the back of a passing taxi or drawing the curtains of an upstairs room" (*Garrick Year*, p. 47). But she understands that the remoteness is essential to the glamour of these situations. Initially attracted to her future husband for his unfamiliar, exotic ways, she was aware of the necessity of keeping him at a psychological distance: "When he tried to tell me about himself I would stop listening: I did not want to know. All I wanted was this feeling of terror with which he inspired me: with him, I felt that I was on the verge of some unknown and frightful land" (*Garrick Year*, p. 29). And, of course, her intuition was correct: marriage to David places him in the light of common day, and the humdrum and familiar replace the mysterious and glamorous.

The imagery of many of the later visions is also introduced in these first two novels. The more desirable existences imagined by Sarah and Emma are associated with works of art. Sarah, for example, envies the life of her rootless, bohemian friend Simone, whom she perceives more as a work of art than as an ordinary human being. Simone's manner, her garb, and even her handwriting are all highly stylized; she "moves through a strange impermanent world where objects are invested with as much power as people, and places possibly with more: these things have for her a pure aesthetic value" (*Bird-Cage*, p. 78). Sarah wistfully notes that this is "totally divorced from the world of sensations and rhythms where I live" (*Bird-Cage*, p. 78), a messy, all too real world of "kitchens and gas-meters and draughts under the door and tiresome quarrels" (*Bird-Cage*, p. 79). Simone, on the contrary, is "cut after an unlivable pattern" (*Bird-Cage*, p. 78), like a work of art.

Emma also displays a longing to escape into the realm of art. The intense, romantic quality of her initial relationship with David having evaporated after their marriage, she hunts for it elsewhere. But of course, reality being what it is, this quality eludes her. Only in a dream—of an idyllic pastoral outing with a lover—does she recapture it. Her dream is "like a scene out of a book, a passion out of a poem, it had all the pure intensity that never occurs in life, the dizzy undistractedness, with no rivers [one of Emma's children has recently almost drowned in a river], no children: so that when I woke I really felt that I had been elsewhere" (*Garrick Year*, p. 203). Such perfection, as Emma acknowledges, lies only in the realm of art, not in that of reality. Indeed, the actual pastoral outing she makes with her family at the end of the novel underscores this fact, for it contains the dangers and dissatisfactions that are noticeably absent from her dream-outing but that are an inevitable part of human life. There are poisonous snakes lurking in the meadow grasses; there are children to worry about; and the marriage between Emma and David is far from ideal, having been dealt a blow by their recent infidelities.

Emma's and Sarah's preference for art over life is only occasional, never assuming the form of a sustained vision. But in Drabble's fourth through eighth novels, vision plays a more prominent role in the protagonists' lives. And in three of these novels, the author explores a type of vision that she elsewhere makes the central subject of a short story. Most of the visions are characterized by either a distinctly artistic or a distinctly mythic quality. Helen, of "A Voyage to Cythera" (1967), a story centered around a vision which, as we shall later see, is strikingly similar to Clara Maugham's, and Jane, of *The Waterfall*, are irresistibly drawn to the realm of art. Helen prefers to stand apart from life, artistically, regarding others' dramas as icons. She draws "faith from the passionate vision of intimacy, where intimacy itself fail[s] her" and understands why Yeats chose to turn from reality to "lions and towers and hawks."[3]

Drabble does her most extensive study of the desire to escape into art in *The Waterfall*. The presentation of the protagonist's vision is more complicated here than in the other works, for it involves the novel's form as well as its content. Jane Gray is a poet who turns from life to art because she finds the former unsatisfying and difficult. As a young child she was acutely aware of life's inadequacies, craving an intensity and clarity in her experiences that life never provides. Her feelings at age seven about her cherished marble collection capture her outlook:

> I always felt myself, with those marbles, to be on the edge of
> some discovery, some activity too delightful to bear, and yet I

could never quite reach it: it always eluded me, and whatever I did—laying them out in rows, looking at them, not looking at them, adding to them, pretending to lose some of them— never quite fulfilled the glorious expectation of having them. I felt there was always something left undone, some final joyful possession of them, some way to have my having of them more completely. I felt this with all games . . . but the moment never happened, it would fade and drop away, . . . each time by-passing its rightful end. (*Waterfall*, pp. 141– 42).

Many Drabble protagonists are haunted by similar feelings, forever searching for a certain situation or place that will embody the heightened significance they are after. Jane looks for it in art—in the magic that language can create.

When we meet her she is a twenty-eight-year-old woman who has become so disenchanted with life that she does the minimum to survive. She has no husband, for she drove him to abandon her shortly before the birth of their second child. She has also stopped seeing friends and given up on her career as a published poet. She pours her energy into art instead of life by writing a highly stylized account of her experience during the year following her husband's desertion, when she has a love affair with her cousin Lucy's husband. The novel is composed of alternating sections of Jane's third-person, fictional narrative and her first-person, nonfictional narrative. The former is consciously artistic—thick with imagery of blood, water, dust, and foliage, and narrated in a heavily cadenced, cumulative style that draws attention to itself:

> And she smiled at him, slowly, deliberately, capitulating, in complicity, assenting, though to what she did not know, and said, "And in the end, then, will you rescue me?"
>
> "Oh yes," he said, touching her knee under the sheet, very gently and carefully touching her knee with his hand. "Oh yes, when it's time, I'll rescue you."
>
> "I'll be so glad of that," she said. "I'll be so grateful for that."
> (*Waterfall*, p. 41)

The heavy, mesmerizing quality of the language reflects the nature of the love it portrays: highly stylized and self-consciously romantic. Drabble has explained that she was trying to depict a sublime, "almost thirteenth-century love."[4] Indeed, like courtly lovers, Jane and James fill their affair with rituals, superstitions, and codes. They have their own "language"—cryptic and oblique, as the above example shows—and their own private universe. Its atmosphere is almost claustrophobic, as though the action were taking place under a bell jar. The lovers are greatly attracted to enclosed places: besides the womblike bedroom, they like being shut up in James' automobile, desiring "to live forever, there in that car" (*Waterfall*, p. 97), and in the hospital room where James convalesces after his accident.

The affair itself did occur: what is fictional is the aura Jane surrounds it with in her third-person narrative. She creates an intense, concentrated atmosphere that cannot be found in real life, where "the multiplicity of objects" (*Waterfall*, p. 78) distracts and disperses one's energies and loyalties. In their airtight world, which the fictional Jane and James feel is "like heaven" (*Waterfall*, p. 39), experience is unified and unambiguous, in contrast to the real world in which it is "a broken and fragmented piece: an event seen from angles" that "don't add up to a whole; they are mutually exclusive: the social view, the sexual view, the circumstantial view, the moral view, these visions contradict each other" (*Waterfall*, pp. 51–52).

Jane, then, is responding to her dissatisfaction with ordinary reality by creating a fictional world that embodies her vision of a more highly charged reality. Whereas the visions of other protagonists often resemble art, Jane's vision actually is a work of art: the fiction she creates. And like much art, it has no moral dimensions or didactic purposes; rather, it is "pointlessly lovely," a phrase Jane often uses in describing various aspects of the affair. Indeed, art rather than truth is what matters in the world she creates. For example, when James tells the fictional Jane that he has always loved her, " 'Ah, rubbish, rubbish, darling, you make it all up, you know I like to hear it,' she said, enchanted, not even caring whether he was lying or telling the truth, quite sufficiently enchanted by the elegance, the tactful charm of the lie" (*Waterfall*, p. 97).

In contrast, in her nonfictional narrative Jane is very much concerned with truth and moral ambiguities, sometimes becoming impatient with her evasive manner in the other account, as when she begins one of her first-person sections with "Lies, lies, it's all lies. A pack of lies" (*Waterfall*, p. 98). Here she explores the difficult issues she would not allow to impinge on the "islanded world" (*Waterfall*, p. 83) of her fiction: the unresolved nature of her marriage; her guilt regarding adultery; her uneasy speculation about how much Lucy

knows of the affair; her doubts about the nature of her love for
James; her frustrations and ambitions regarding her career. The
form as well as the content of the nonfictional sections is bathed in
the "coarser air" (*Waterfall*, p. 99) of ordinary reality, in contrast to
the distilled air of the fictional world. In particular, the language is
transparent and referential, pointing to a real, exterior world,
rather than creating a mosaic of words and images, as it does in the
other narrative.

It is in this way — by sustaining herself through an artistic vision —
that Jane copes with the inadequacy and difficulty of life. Although
her withdrawal from living and absorption in art is for a while taken
to an unhealthy extreme, this eventually proves to have been a
salutary experience, for she is ultimately able to reengage with life by
integrating the artistic vision with ordinary existence. The final
episode of the book, Jane and James' excursion to Goredale Scar,
indicates this change. Their outing contains some sublime moments — Jane feels inspiration and poetry while gazing down at the
waterfall — but also some ridiculous, very human moments — later, in
their hotel room, a potentially romantic evening is suddenly undercut by James' gagging on a mug of whisky into which Jane earlier
accidentally spilled talcum powder. Jane, who in the earlier stages of
the relationship would not have been able to describe these two
incidents in the same narrative, can now smile and wryly remark,
"Scotch and dust. A fitting conclusion to the sublimities of nature"
(*Waterfall*, p. 289).

In 1968, the year before *The Waterfall* came out, Drabble published
a story which appears to be a foreshadowing of this novel. Variously
titled "The Reunion" and "Faithful Lovers," it is about a pair of
lovers who closely resemble Jane and James in the novel's fictional
account.[5] Like their counterparts, they are married to others, and
like most Drabble protagonists, they find life bleak. The woman
reflects that her existence is filled with tedium and "anxieties, which
had existed before him, and which would exist forever, because they
were what she was made of. Inadequacy, loneliness, panic, vanity,
decay" ("Reunion," p. 152). The action consists of their accidental
meeting at the café they had frequented during their love affair,
which terminated three years earlier although they were and still are
in love with each other.

Their attitude toward the affair suggests that it functions primarily as a vision, sustaining them in their dark lives. They invest it with
the kind of magic and significance other Drabble protagonists attach

to their visions. This one most particularly resembles Jane's as depicted in her fictional narrative. Like the fictional Jane and James, these lovers create an enclosed, romantic world of their own, shut off from the real world. Whereas Jane and James' world exists primarily in Jane's bedroom, this couple's exists in the café. Their visionary world is charged with an intensity not found in the real one. All the objects in the café, from the plastic containers on the tables to the tatty calender on the wall, are curiously important to them, taking on a special meaning because of the significance that charges the room. The woman has memorized all the physical details of the café and cannot bear for any of them to be changed.

Again like Jane and James, this couple has developed a ritualistic way of conversing—"their own studiously developed amorous dialect" ("Reunion," p. 167), a "charmed and passionate dialogue" ("Reunion," p. 162). They too elevate their relationship to the level of high romance: as Jane compares James and herself with Tristram and Isolde and with Cupid and Psyche, so this woman compares her lover and herself with Paolo and Francesca. Finally, they share with other Drabble protagonists the sense that their vision has been dictated by fate. For this reason, they submit to their passion, "unresisting, finally unresisting, as though three years of solitude had been nothing but a pause, nothing but a long breath before this final acknowledgement of nature, damnation, and destiny . . . because they believed in such things, because that was what they believed in, because, like disastrous romantics, they habitually connived with fate by remembering the names of restaurants and the streets they had once walked as lovers" ("Reunion," p. 168).

Strangely, the possibility of leaving their spouses for each other is never entertained, causing one to suspect that they do not want to transfer their relationship to the real world for fear it would lose its glamour. This attitude is characteristic of most Drabble protagonists, who recognize the essentially elusive nature of their visions and allow them to function as inspirations rather than actual goals.

In "Crossing the Alps" (1971), Drabble again uses the kind of highly romantic situation she employs in *The Waterfall* and "The Reunion." Two lovers, unhappily married to others, plan a secret holiday from reality, thinking that "all they needed for entire felicity was a few days together, with light and air, away from that depressing flat and [the woman's retarded] child, away from her depressing work, away from his own depressing wife" ("Alps," p. 155). But they are never given the chance to test their vision because the man becomes ill with flu as they set off for the Alps and has to be nursed the rest of the trip. Disappointed though they are, the situation gives rise to compensatory revelations about the power of the imagination, not unlike the experience Wordsworth describes in Book VI of *The Prelude*, and hence the story's title. The woman points out, "don't you see, my love, that we simply haven't a *chance* of being given a chance? It's wonderful, really. It's miraculous. Even now . . . when we did have a bit of a chance, you've gone and got this horrible illness, so we'll never know what it would have been like if you hadn't. We'll never have to worry about it, we can just carry on being kind, and making promises. It's amazing, really. There'll never be any reason to know that we couldn't do it" ("Alps," p. 198).

Their trip, then, does not bring them the kind of fulfillment they had desired—attainment of perfect felicity; on the contrary, it has made them realize that such happiness is probably impossible. However, their Wordsworthian insight provides them with the kind of philosophical happiness described in "Tintern Abbey" and the "Immortality Ode." Although the "visionary gleam" is forever beyond their grasp, they find joy in their imagination of it.

Whereas in *The Waterfall* and its related stories the vision is of a more highly charged emotional existence, in *Jerusalem the Golden* it is social as well as emotional in nature, and it resembles both a work of art and a mythic golden city. This novel also has a thematic counterpart in a short story. "A Voyage to Cythera," published in the same year as the novel (1967), presents in condensed, concentrated form the same type of vision. Helen, the story's protagonist, is, like Clara, obsessed with the thinness of her own life and envisions one of social and emotional complexity. The story centers around one such flight of her imagination, revealing the extent to which vision preoccupies her. Travelling home on the train one evening after work, she finds herself seated across from a strange, romantic-looking man who begins perusing in harassed distraction what appear to be love letters. Helen's rich imagination latches onto this scene and begins conjuring up all sorts of attractive possibilities about his situation. Her curiosity is further aroused when he composes a note, places it in an envelope, and then timorously asks her if she wouldn't mind addressing and later posting it. Assenting, she is delighted to discover—because it enhances the intrigue—that the woman is married: "Mrs. H. Smithson." When the train reaches its destination, the two strangers bid each other adieu and go their separate ways, Helen posting the letter on her way home.

But this is not the end of the experience for her: "over the next month, she sometimes fancied that she thought of little else" ("Voyage," p. 148). Her own drab, sterile life—consisting of little more than a humdrum job, a bare flat, and visits to her mother—pales further into insignificance as she contemplates the richness and intrigue of the strange man's and Mrs. Smithson's lives. Finally, one cold snowy afternoon just before Christmas, she feels compelled to go and have a look at Mrs. Smithson's house, having memorized the address from the envelope. Her musings as she sets off on her trek suggest the mythical nature of her vision of a more desirable life. She feels that she is

> surrendering to the lure of that fraught, romantic, painful world, which seemed to call her, to call her continually from the endurable sorrows of daily existence to some possible other country of the passions, a country where she felt she would recognize, though strange to it, the scenery and landmarks. She thought often of this place, as of some place perpetually existing, and yet concealed: and could describe it to herself only in terms of myth or allegory. . . . It was a world other than the real world, or what she felt to be the real world, and it was both more beautiful and more valid, though valid in itself only: and it could be entered not at will, but intermittently, by accident, and yet always with some sense of temptation and surrender. Some people, she could see, passed most of their lives in its confines. . . . There were enough of such people in the world to keep alive before her the possibility of a permanent, irreversible entry through those mysteriously inscribed and classic gates. ("Voyage," p. 149)

At the end of her musings she sighs to herself, "Oh, messages from a foreign country, oh, disquieting glimpses of brightness" ("Voyage," p. 149).

Arriving at her destination, she discovers that there is a bus stop located directly across the street from Mrs. Smithson's, from where she can inconspicuously gaze into the woman's living room. What she sees going on there—two women animatedly conversing and laying out the tea table while their small children decorate a Christmas tree—is less important than the atmosphere in which Helen perceives the scene to be bathed—one of brightness, magic, and ineffable beauty. She is profoundly affected by this spectacle, and her response reveals her intuition that this vision represents an ideal realm, one she can glimpse but never attain:

> And as she stood there, out there in the cold, and watched, she felt herself stiffen slowly into the breathlessness of attention: because it seemed to her that she had been given, freely, a vision of something so beautiful that its relevance could not be measured. The hints and arrows that had led her here took on the mysterious significance of fate itself: she felt that everything was joined and drawn together, that all things were part of some pattern of which she caught by sheer chance a sudden hopeful sense: and that those two women, and their children, and the man on the train, and the bright and radiant uncurtained room, an island in the surrounding darkness, were symbols to her of things too vague to name, of happiness, of hope, of brightness, warmth, and celebration. ("Voyage," p. 150)

This picture of Helen standing out in the cold, dark night, enthralled by a vision of brightness, is emblematic of the psychological situation of all Drabble protagonists. That Helen does not attempt to bridge the gap between vision and reality by knocking and entering the house reveals her awareness that the vision must be kept at a distance in order to continue to satisfy her imagination. The narrator explains, "She knew nothing, and could therefore believe everything, drawing faith from such a vision, as she had drawn faith from unfamiliar cities" ("Voyage," p. 150). It even occurs to her that she may be serving the same purpose for the strange man she met on the train that he is serving for her: acting as "some mysterious apparition, some faintly gleaming memorable image" ("Voyage," p. 150). Both her suspicion that her vision is tied up with a mysterious other-worldly realm, or fate, and her awareness of its fragile, elusive nature are characteristic of the visions of all Drabble protagonists.

Clara Maugham's vision closely resembles Helen's. Both women crave a life filled with complex, intriguing relationships, with emotional riches and frissons. Clara's need, like Jane's and, as shall be shown, Rose's, developed in early childhood as a result of emotional deprivation. Dissatisfied with the narrow, colorless atmosphere of her home, she was deeply attracted to any suggestion of a richer, more passionate life. She therefore latched onto the image of Jerusalem the Golden in the hymn of that title. However, "she pictured, even at a most tender age, not the pearly gates and crystal walls and golden towers of some heavenly city, but some truly terrestrial paradise, where beautiful people in beautiful houses spoke of beautiful things" (*Jerusalem*, p. 39).

Her life from then on is ruled by the search for such a paradise: she catches glimpses of it in literature, in a school trip to Paris, and, later, in brief romantic encounters with men. But not until she meets the Denham family while a university student in London does she feel she has found the real thing. Again like Helen, as well as other protagonists, she believes that fate has directed her to this vision: "Sometimes she wondered what would have happened if she had missed [the Denhams], and whether a conjunction so fateful and fruitful could have been, by some accidental obtuseness on her part, avoided: she did not like to think so, she liked to think that inevitability had had her in its grip" (*Jerusalem*, p. 12). In fact, she would have found it fitting if upon her introduction to Clelia, the first of the Denhams she met, "a sudden lightning had descended: if she could have said then, this is the kind of thing I have been looking for, and if this is not it, then it is nowhere else" (*Jerusalem*, p. 12).

Throughout the course of her friendship with the Denhams, Clara relegates them to the realm of vision. Sometimes she conceives of their life as a work of art, as when she mentions upon leaving their house that she feels as though she has spent the afternoon in an art gallery. Other times she clothes them in the imagery of paradise and golden worlds, calling them "radiant," "dazzling," "saint-like." She shrinks from any suggestion that the Denhams are ordinary mortals. For example, she is disturbed when she meets Annunciata, the youngest Denham daughter, and notes that her manner is strikingly similar to Clelia's, for this detracts from the uniqueness with which she has endowed Clelia and suggests that the Denhams' style — Annunciata's anyway — may be merely affectation rather than "the real thing" (*Jerusalem*, p. 199). And when she embarks on an affair with Gabriel Denham, she does not want to know the details of his personal life and marriage, for she "[likes] the unknown, she [likes] to feel familiar with the unknown" (*Jerusalem*, p. 181).

Clara, therefore, realizes, as do Helen and Emma, that one must maintain a certain psychological distance from the object of one's vision in order for it to continue to operate as such. As a young child she absorbed this truth from a fable, "The Golden Windows," about a little boy who sees from a hillside a house with golden windows and searches in vain for this wonderful edifice, only to discover when returning home that the house was his own and the gold merely the reflection of the sun. Although Clara realized that the moral of the story was that "one must see the beauty in what one has, and not search for it elsewhere," she was more impressed by "the real sadness of the fading windows, and the fact that those within the house could never see them shine" (*Jerusalem*, p. 41). She therefore must remain a psychological outsider to the Denham household in order to perceive its radiance. The novel ends with her looking forward to a visionary future, "a tender blurred world where Clelia and Gabriel and she herself in shifting and ideal conjunctions met and drifted and met once more like the constellations in the heavens: a bright and peopled world, thick with starry inhabitants" (*Jerusalem*, pp. 238–39). In the immediate future lies an intriguing automobile trip with Gabriel, in which they will speed along the motorway through the night, one of the "lights in the surrounding darkness" (*Jerusalem*, p. 239). This final image reveals the central purpose the Denham vision serves for Clara: it is a hopeful light in the midst of life's darkness, just as for Helen Mrs. Smithson's life is "an island in the surrounding darkness."

In *The Needle's Eye* the vision assumes a moral form: Rose is in search of grace, which she believes can be found in a life of poverty and monastic renunciation of the world's vanities. But although her vision takes a different form from those of other protagonists, it has the same mythic imagery associated with it and fulfills the same psychological need. Rose's religious motives for choosing a life of poverty have already been discussed, but there are additional reasons why this way of life appeals to her. As a child in a cold, wealthy home, she developed a strong attachment to an image of a cozy, working-class domestic life, which she found embodied in the family of a little school friend. This child's father was a cobbler and her mother "a big woman in a flowery apron" (*Needle's Eye*, p. 107). Drabble has illuminated Rose's psychology by explaining, "the persons whom I partly modeled Rose on says she got it [her desire for a cozy, working-class domestic life] from her nanny in the true upper-class British way. She found heaven as a sort of big tatty old arm chair and a woman ironing, while, in her case, her brilliant mother chatted away upstairs to her friends, or so I imagine it."[6] Like Drabble's friend, Rose has a deeply rooted emotional attachment to this image of happiness.

It is of course not unusual for an adult to strive for a goal formed in childhood. But Rose's vision is more than an ordinary goal, as the imagery reveals. Its association in her mind with a holy or golden city suggests the magical, intensely charged quality of the life she craves. And just as Clara's vision was created out of the image suggested to her by "Jerusalem the Golden," so Rose's developed during a period of her life when she was highly susceptible to such mythological pictures. During her early formative years she was greatly attracted to a certain fairy tale about a prince and princess, and endlessly reenacted the story with her little school friend. She was particularly affected by the word "yonder," which they had occasion to use frequently in their make-believe dialogue. Rose recalls the awe and power that word held for her: it "would evoke a place of such mystic and visionary loveliness, a thin aspiring castle on the brow of a green hill, a tower above the raging sea, a heavenly city" (*Needle's Eye*, p. 107). This childlike image of a glorious, elusive realm of existence made a deep psychological imprint on her and became the heart of her governing vision.

Rose's vision is to a certain extent attainable: she successfully creates for a time the cozy, shabby, charitable life she desires. But the magical, transcendent quality that is the essence of a vision floods Rose's life only occasionally, for this quality is at odds with human reality. Although Rose in a sense achieves her vision, only in fleeting moments does she fully live in this "holy city." During one such moment she reflects on both the nature of her vision and the difficulty of sustaining it:

> Fleas, holes, cold, single eggs. Behind these threatening entities there loomed a shadowy edifice, an inhabited house, a hope for the future; she shivered, she trembled, she flinched, but she persevered, she had faith, she built up brick by brick the holy city of her childhood, the holy city in the shape of that patched subsiding house. It was slow, it was very slow, but gradually the ideal and the real merged and swam together, so that there were times, when, after five years or so, she would sit there not knowing which she inhabited, irritated at one moment beyond measure by the noise of the radio next door and the fraying edge of the carpet and the way the cats had ripped the braid off the armchairs, and the next moment invaded by such visionary peace at her acceptance of and familiarity with these things. Her alliance with the objects around had irradiated her, transformed her. But her friends, or such friends as continued, through loyalty or love or

curiosity or desire for profit to make the long journey, continued to think that she was mad. Hardly a gleam of her vision reached them. (*Needle's Eye*, pp. 53–54)

Rose thus vacillates between inhabiting the real and inhabiting the ideal, but increasingly reality overwhelms her. She can finally no longer withstand her former husband's pressuring her to take him back, although she knows that in doing so she is, as Ellen Cronan Rose effectively puts it, "[turning] from her state of quasi-grace toward a messy reality of domestic bickering, confused loyalties, and mixed priorities."[7] The contingencies of reality force her vision into the recesses of her mind; reluctantly she watches "heaven . . . [being] taken slowly from her, as its bright gleams [fade]" (*Needle's Eye*, p. 365). But although her life no longer coincides so closely with her vision, Rose has intermittent joyful moments when the latter returns. The novel ends with such a moment—when she accompanies Simon, Emily, and their various children on an afternoon's outing to shabby Alexandra Palace, a situation reminiscent of her old life. Rose's vision, then, like all Drabble visions, is finally unattainable, because it belongs to the realm of myth, art, and the imagination; but it can descend upon her at certain moments, brightening her dark existence.

Simon too is affected by a vision, although his is derivative: he is the one friend of Rose's whom a "gleam of her vision" does reach. When we first meet him he is a spiritually dry, middle-aged man, his life all darkness and grim duty. He is convinced that "there [is] no light, or none that man might enter" (*Needle's Eye*, p. 172). He is, in fact, ripe for receiving a vision, which comes to him in the form of Rose, to whom he is introduced at a party. From the beginning he regards her with the awe Drabble protagonists have for their visions, associating her and her life with golden, celestial imagery. Sitting talking with her in her shabby living room the first night of their acquaintance, he feels himself in the midst of an "intimate, redeeming, cluttered pool of light" (*Needle's Eye*, p. 44). An image of a bright enclosed place filled with magic or grace, irradiating the dark night, is of course one that Drabble often uses in presenting visions. Simon also comes to associate Rose and her life with a work of art. Ellen Cronan Rose astutely observes, "When he first meets her, he slips almost immediately from accurate observation to iconography," likening her looks to ancient frescoes.[8]

Indeed, Rose is more important to Simon as symbol or vision than as person. He maintains her in this status by not becoming too intimate with her; this in part explains why he chooses not to marry her although he is in love with her. Like so many Drabble protagonists, he prefers to dream about an ideal life rather than attempt it and have it dissolve into the ordinary. Instead, Rose remains a symbolic hope that helps him endure his bleak life. Depending so completely on this vision for spiritual sustenance, he is fearful of anything that threatens to diminish its magic or power. Hence, he does not want Rose to change in any way; after she takes back Christopher he is afraid she may lose her saintly aspect and descend to the level of ordinary mortal: "He watched. He watched like a hawk, for signs of cracking, for signs of ruin, for signs of decay. He needed her, he needed her more than ever. He watched her clothes, to see if she would spend money on herself. He watched her hair, to see if she would have it done, at three guineas a time. He watched her face, and the lines of it, to see if she would betray him" (*Needle's Eye*, p. 358). Even the objects and trappings associated with her life are symbolically important to him: "He watched the inside of her house, the rooms of it, the rooms she lived in. Breathlessly, over the years, he watched. They changed, a little. They did not change much. Such love, such salvation, he felt, at the sight of each object that remained in its place. The tea caddy. The tin tray. The armchair. The shabby cat" (*Needle's Eye*, p. 359).

In the final episode of the book, the outing to Alexandra Palace, Simon as well as Rose is flooded with visionary grace. As he watches her ascend the monument's stairs, he suddenly perceives her transformed by a celestial light:

> her hair itself, falling on to the points of her fur collar, fell into a thousand bright individual fiery sparks, the hair and the fur meeting, radiant, luminous, catching whatever fell from the sun upon them, stirring like living threads in the sea into a phosphorescent life, turning, and lifting, alive on the slight breeze of her walking, a million lives from the dead beasts, a million from her living head, haloed there, a million shining in a bright and dazzling outline, a million in one. She walked ahead, encircled by brightness. (*Needle's Eye*, pp. 362–63)

The vision fades, but Simon has once again been spiritually nourished; with deep satisfaction he reflects that "he would look forward to hearing, over the months and years, the things that she

would have to say" (*Needle's Eye*, p. 367) — an understated but revealing comment on the important function Rose performs in his life.

In a short story published six years earlier, "Hassan's Tower"
(1966), Drabble created a protagonist who prefigures Simon
Camish. Kenneth, a young Englishman on his honeymoon in
Morocco, is suffering from a spiritual bitterness and disillusionment
similar to that which burdens Simon at the beginning of *The Needle's
Eye*. He too has become disenchanted with his marriage but knows
that he will stick by his wife out of duty. The prospect of a long, bleak
life of endurance and little beauty fills him with heavy depression.
Like Simon, then, he is ripe for a redeeming vision. While on an
excursion to the top of Hassan's Tower, he experiences a sudden
revelation that unveils the significance and beauty hidden in ordinary human reality:

> as he gazed he felt growing within him a sense of extraordi-
> nary familiarity that was in its own way a kind of illumination,
> for he saw all these foreign people keenly lit with a visionary
> gleam of meaning. . . . He saw these people, quite suddenly,
> for what they were, for people, for nothing but or other than
> people; their clothes filled out with bodies, their faces took on
> expression, their relations became dazzlingly clear, as though
> the details of their strangeness had dropped away, as though
> the terms of common humanity (always before credited in
> principle, but never before perceived) had become facts be-
> fore his eyes. . . . And it seemed to him that it was not he
> himself that was for the first time seeing, but rather that
> perception had descended upon him, like a gift, like a sign,
> like a bird. He could see: he wanted to cry out that he could
> see, and that five minutes earlier he had resigned himself to
> blindness. And the vision before him now was of a promise
> and a hope far fuller than any of the passions of his youth,
> because it was no longer a lonely knowledge: it had a hundred
> different faces. The world was not empty, as he had feared.[9]

Although Kenneth, like Simon, will probably not change anything
external in his life as a result of the vision, it has served to make his
otherwise dark existence bearable. One can imagine his dreary
future being lit up by such occasional experiences.

Again in "The Gifts of War" (1970), Drabble shows how a vision
can sustain one through a depressing marriage. Maternal love, always a source of profound fulfillment for Drabble women, is the

door to visionary insights for this protagonist. The one redeeming factor in the woman's bleak existence is her love for her young son; it provides her with faith in the significance and beauty of life, despite its apparent meaninglessness and ugliness. Like Rosamund of *The Millstone*, she feels that the experience of maternal love has made her "one of the elected few, [who have] been permitted to glimpse something of the very nature of the harsh, mysterious processes of human survival: and she could induce in herself a state of recognition that was almost visionary" ("Gifts," p. 28). Motherhood has given her "a kind of superior wisdom, a higher order of knowledge" ("Gifts," p. 28). It is the one redeeming factor in her drab life: "She fed off it: her maternal role" ("Gifts," p. 28).

Whereas in *Jerusalem the Golden* and *The Needle's Eye* the image of a golden city is a metaphor for the protagonists' visions, in *The Realms of Gold* it figures literally as well as figuratively: Frances, as an archaeologist, actually discovers and excavates such a city, the ancient site of the Tizouk civilization in the Sahara. She is of course immensely proud of her accomplishment for professional reasons; but her more significant satisfactions from it are emotional and spiritual. Knowing that such a civilization existed—a healthy, cultured, spiritual civilization—helps ward off the existential despair that frequently grips her, convincing her of "the absolute futility of all human effort" (*Realms*, p. 222). The discovery of Tizouk helps fill her need to believe in a Golden Age. Indeed, it was this very need that caused her to take up archaeology in the first place. In one of her moments of despair and cynicism, she observes that her pursuit of archaeology and her lover Karel's of history is nothing more than "a fruitless attempt to prove the possibility of the future through the past. We seek a utopia in the past, a possible if not an ideal society. We seek golden worlds from which we are banished, they recede infinitely, for there never was a golden world, there was never anything but toil and subsistence, cruelty and dullness" (*Realms*, pp. 120–21).

Frances, thus, suspects that "the realms of gold" are a myth; like other Drabble protagonists she realizes that her vision has more to do with the imagination than with reality. In fact, she mentally refers to Tizouk as "the city of her imagination" (*Realms*, p. 27). This epithet has two levels of meaning: Tizouk is the city of her imagination in that she intuited, or imagined, that it existed and then went and excavated for it; but it is also the city of her imagination in that she has imaginatively endowed it with visionary glory. Reflecting on the power of her imagination, Frances muses, "I imagine a city, and it exists. If I hadn't imagined it, it wouldn't have existed. . . . What next should she imagine? What terrifying enormity should she next conjure forth? Should she dig again in the desert and uncover gold? Should she plant down her foot and let water spring from the dry land? Should she wave her arm and let the rocks blossom?" (*Realms*, p. 29). It is ultimately her imagination that spiritually nourishes Frances and enables her to affirm life. As Carey Kaplan points out, *The Realms of Gold* is a celebration of the power of the imagination, in particular of its ability to give meaning and beauty to the raw, chaotic materials of life.

Further evidence that for Frances Tizouk is more significant as a vision than as an actual city is the mystery and magic in which she enshrouds her discovery. She senses that it was divinely inspired; like Clara, she feels that fate directed her to it. Why, she wonders with awe, "had she been allowed to know? . . . It was so arbitrary, it had frightened her terribly. She had known that the city was there, she had gone out to dig for it, and she had found it. But all because of one flash of knowledge. Where had it come from, and why had she been allowed to have it, that revelation on which so much depended?" (*Realms*, p. 28). Frances sounds here as though she were describing a religious conversion, and in a sense her discovery is similar to one, for it provides her with a vision that spiritually sustains her as she plods through the rubble of modern civilization.

Although the subject of Karel Schmidt's vision is not directly addressed in the novel, there is indication that he too suffers from a sense of futility and craves a greater intensity and significance to his life. Like certain other protagonists, in particular Jane as a child, he has moments of feeling himself on the verge of such an experience, but it never materializes:

> From time to time, through the years, through a lifetime of endeavor, he had felt welling up in him a kind of compelled and induced love, and had felt as though he were on the brink of a discovery so wonderful that all the doubts and hours of boredom and inadequate responses [to the pathetic, lonely students he has taken under his wing] would be justified: Mrs. Mayfield or Dick Wilkie would suddenly bask in his unforced, real, shining love, and would at last be made whole. . . . But the vision would fade, and he would be forced to see himself in the light of common day: weak, overidentifying with the

unlovely, unable to say no, with a peculiar capacity for enduring hours and hours of unremitting boredom. (*Realms*, pp.
90–91)

The Ice Age's Anthony Keating also possesses a visionary bent. Like
the other protagonists, he hungers for a greater intensity and significance than ordinary reality provides. He ultimately finds these
qualities in religious life, as has been shown, but at an earlier stage of
his life he experienced another kind of "conversion"—from liberal
intellectual to capitalist. As dissimilar—and even opposite—as his
two conversions are, they spring from the same psychological need:
the need to escape ordinary reality by imaginatively endowing it with
a significance or purpose he has not customarily perceived. Just as
Rose Vassiliou introduces into Simon's life a much-needed vision, so
Len Wincobank, property development tycoon, does the same for
Anthony. But whereas Simon was suffering from spiritual dryness,
Anthony's was primarily intellectual:

> He would wake up in the middle of the night and think: Is this
> it? Is what what? In short, he was underemployed, bored, and
> not at all happy in his relation to his work, his country, or the
> society he lived in: ripe for conversion, to some new creed. A
> political creed, but there wasn't one; a religious creed, but he
> had had God, along with his [minister] father and life in the
> cathedral close. So what would happen to the vacant spot in
> Anthony Keating? What would occupy it? (*Ice Age*, p. 21)

It is during this phase of his life that he reviews, in his job as
television producer, a taped interview with Len Wincobank. Although at first dismissing the businessman's views as uninspired
and immorally pragmatic, on running the tape through a second
time he is struck "suddenly, with a dazzling flash" (*Ice Age*, p. 22),
by their brilliance and excitement. This is the beginning of Anthony's "conversion" to capitalism, and it leads him to give up his
old career and start a property development company. But it is
clear from the beginning that his motive is not crass greed; rather,
he is attracted by the romance and intellectual excitement of land
speculation. His attitude is more like a religious convert's than a
business tycoon's: he refers to the insight Len has given him as a
"revelation" (*Ice Age*, p. 23), and, as for a religious convert the
world is suddenly made beautiful by God's love where before it
had been meaningless or ugly, so for Anthony

London became a changed place. . . . Before, he had seen it
as a system of roads linking the houses of friends and the
places of his employment, with a few restaurants and shops
included in his personal map: now he began to see it as a
dense and lively forest of possibilities. Whole areas,
hitherto neglected, acquired significance. At first Anthony
went around dazed by achievements that he had once taken
for granted: what genius had assembled the land for Bowa-
ter House, for Eastbourne Terrace in Paddington, for soar-
ing Millbank Tower and elegant Castrol House? (*Ice Age*, p.
26)

In *The Ice Age*, as in *The Realms of Gold*, the vision of a golden
city takes on a literal as well as mythical form. London becomes a
glorious, shining place to Anthony, a magical city of infinite (real
estate) possibilities—Anthony's version of the child Rose's "yonder" land. He endows his vision with the same kind of radiance
the other protagonists do theirs. For instance, transformed by his
visionary regard, a gasometer he purchases becomes something
transcendent and sublime:

It was painted a steely gray-blue, and it rose up against the
sky like a part of the sky itself; iron air, a cloud, a mirage, a
paradox, defining a space of sky, changing subtly in color
as the color of the sky changed. It stood dark and cold, it
would catch the pink wash of sunset, it would turn white
like a sea gull, it would take upon itself the delicate palest
blue against a slate-dark background. It was a work of
art. . . . Anthony would gaze upon it with more pride and
more wonder than he had ever, in his childhood, regarded
the cathedral outside his bedroom window. . . . A derelict
gasometer, radiant with significance. (*Ice Age*, pp. 27–28)

Anthony's new London is a city of his imagination in the same way
that Tizouk is for Frances. And both Anthony and Frances imply
an awareness of the essentially imaginative nature of their visions
when they voice their fears that the whole thing is a fantasy. Just
as Frances sometimes "thought that it was all an elaborate mistake, and that she would wake up one morning and discover that
the city was not there, and had never been there" (*Realms*, p. 29),
so Anthony at first frequently revisits the site where his new property company will be housed, "to reassure himself that the whole

enterprise was real, not a mere fantasy" (*Ice Age*, p. 26). Perhaps *The Ice Age* more than any of the other novels reveals the primary place of the imagination in the protagonists' visions, for Anthony's vision is quite clearly a product of his imagination: the city London, in its phenomenal reality, has not changed; instead, Anthony's imagination has imposed significance and glory upon it. The fact that in this book the raw material of the vision is the most pedestrian—literally, bricks and mortar—further underscores its essentially imaginative nature. And finally, Anthony's ultimate conversion to a spiritual outlook is not inconsistent with, or a reaction against, his previous embrace of the world of mammon. Rather, both are manifestations of the same psychological impulse: the need to transform phenomenal reality, by means of the imagination, into something transcendent and beautiful.

Drabble's most recent protagonist, *The Middle Ground*'s Kate Armstrong, is not preoccupied with a vision to the extent that many earlier protagonists are. The most practical and least spiritual of the protagonists, she nonetheless at times inclines to a mystical outlook. For example, when she learns of her accidental pregnancy, she interprets it as "a visitation, an offer that [can] not be rejected" (*Middle Ground*, p. 65) and feels that "she [has] been chosen for the burden, she [can] not lay it down" (*Middle Ground*, p. 70). Here Kate, ordinarily not religious, is attracted to the comforting idea of a God who oversees all human activity. Another time she voices to her friend Hugo a personal theory she has worked out to account for her intuition of a realm beyond phenomenal reality:

> I sometimes think . . . that we are all of us living other lives, kind of just out of sight, just round the corner from our conscious lives, that if you were to roll it all up together, your life and mine, the lived and the unlived, it would be something quite different, a whole life, not a half-life, many whole lives, the shadows of our own as they roll along, and perhaps this one, you and me sitting here, is just the shadow of what we are doing elsewhere, in some other world, in some other part of our being. I can't believe that this is all. Us at this table. How can it be all? (*Middle Ground*, pp. 259–60)

As Simon Camish catches the gleams of Rose Vassiliou's vision, so Hugo does of Kate's. Gazing at her while she explains her theory, he observes that "at such moments something in Kate seemed to shimmer just beneath or above the surface, *sub limen*, a breaking light, and she had this knack, this gift, for catching a little of it and bringing it, but just, but just within range, like an astral halo flickering on the sight, calling from him a corresponding gleam: a bright person, an angel in the house, among the crumbs and dustbins and fish heads" (*Middle Ground*, p. 260). But as is typical of Drabble visions, this one is difficult to sustain for more than a brief moment. One always fall back into one's customary perceptions: "Ah, folly, thought Hugo, as he watched, she is just a woman, and a rather gullible, foolish, self-centered, vain woman at that" (*Middle Ground*, p. 260).

Although visions are fleeting and infrequent in *The Middle Ground*, the novel nonetheless upholds their importance. It concludes with Kate's experiencing a Woolfian epiphany similar to Clarissa's at the end of *Mrs. Dalloway*. As does her fictional predecessor's, Kate's party takes on a supernatural significance, becoming a celebration of the transcendent beauty to be found in life and in human relationships. As Kate prepares for the festivity, she feels a mystical connection with her family, her friends, her life, and her future: "Excitement fills her, excitement, joy, anticipation, apprehension. Something will happen. The water glints in the distance. It is unplanned, unpredicted. Nothing binds her, nothing holds her. It is the unknown, and there is no way of stopping it. It waits, unseen, and she will meet it, it will meet her. There is no way of knowing what it will be. It does not know itself. But it will come into being. A child calls her from downstairs. The doorbell rings. The telephone also rings. She hears her house living. She rises" (*Middle Ground*, p. 277).

Vision, thus, plays an important role in the lives of Drabble's protagonists, offering them hope and nourishing their spirits and imaginations. Some of these visions are more obviously spiritual than others, to the point of being virtually the same as religious faith; the others, while not directly associated with God or religion, nonetheless possess a mystical quality. Even the most secular of visions—such as Clara's of an exciting social and emotional life—appear to have been sent by fate. Drabble herself uses religious and spiritual terminology to describe the revelations and visionary moments of her characters. She believes that during such times one is in a "state of grace," "in tune with the purpose of life" or "with some other purpose." She goes on to explain that grace "descends from heaven like the muse" and that "by accident you happen to fall into it, or stumble into it, or it happens to descend upon you like a kind of bird from the sky."[10] Of course, we know from what Drabble has said elsewhere that she believes all accidents and coincidences are really part of some larger, divine plan. She has also said that she believes in the human soul, but that only occasionally does one have a sense of one's soul and of acting in accordance with it. These are the "moments of real significance in one's life," "moment[s] of revelation, or vision, or integration," of "love, or illumination, or even of thought."[11]

Drabble's notions about this subject are, as she admits, vague; they stem from idiosyncratic mystical tendencies rather than a particular theology. But it is clear that she regards the visionary leanings of her protagonists in a positive light. Although one could argue that attachment to a vision is an unhealthy, escapist response to one's unhappiness with life, or, as Ellen Cronan Rose suggests, that it is a sign of immature idealism, Drabble does not take either view. Her outlook is so fatalistic that she believes that, rather than try to change the world, people should snatch at whatever happiness or means of coping they can find. Vision not only enables one to cope but also enriches one's spiritual and imaginative life by its suggestion of an order of reality removed from the customary mundane one. Although Drabble explores the problems an obsessive vision can give rise to—for example, the conflicts it creates in Rose's marriage and the way it allows Jane to withdraw for a time from living—she never has her characters ultimately renounce their visions. Instead, they learn to balance them with other, worldly concerns. Only in *Jerusalem the Golden* does Drabble appear to treat the protagonist's vision ironically. But her attitude here is mixed. She sympathizes with and approves of Clara's search for a more meaningful "pattern of life" but says that "in the book I have ambivalent feelings myself about whether she's found a good one. Clearly not. She's found something that suits her. She's going to turn into something fearsome, I think. I rather dread her future."[12]

Drabble regards the need for vision as a demonstration of the power of the human imagination and spirit, which all her fiction ultimately celebrates. Although she was referring specifically to *The Needle's Eye*, her statement "one of the themes I was trying to explore was the possibility of living, today, without faith, a religious life"[13] can be applied to all her fiction. Only Rose Vassiliou and

Anthony Keating are religious in the strict sense of the word, but all her protagonists believe in a transcendent significance beyond phenomenal, quotidian reality. It matters not whether they believe the visionary gleam is an emanation from heaven or whether they suspect it is a "city of their imagination"; either way, their attachment to this "light in the surrounding darkness" redeems, and injects moments of beauty into, their bleak lives.

6

Imagination: The Role of Literature

Literature as well as vision holds an important position in Drabble's theory of the imagination. One of the most prominent features of her fiction is her heavy use of traditional literary references and echoes, as the following survey will indicate.[1]

The titles of many of the novels allude to older literature: *A Summer Bird-Cage* to John Webster's lines, " 'Tis just like a summer bird cage in a garden, the birds that are without despair to get in, and the birds that are within despair and are in a consumption for fear they shall never get out"; *The Millstone* and *The Needle's Eye* to Biblical passages; *Jerusalem the Golden* to the hymn of that title by J. M. Neale; and *The Realms of Gold* to a line in Keats' sonnet "On First Looking into Chapman's Homer."[2] Even the names of the protagonists—especially Emma, Rosamund, and Jane—remind us of the heroines of nineteenth-century British novels. And many of the scenes and episodes have analogues in older literature. For example, Drabble has claimed that *Middlemarch* provided her with the idea for the relationship between the two sisters in *A Summer Bird-Cage*.[3] Indeed, the passage in Drabble's novel in which the older sister visits a cathedral in Italy while on her honeymoon is strikingly similar to that in Eliot's describing Dorothea Brooke's parallel experience. Both women are observed unawares by acquaintances who are struck by their stony, resigned appearances, indicative of their attitudes toward their marriages.

Drabble has also mentioned that scenes from Arnold Bennett's *Hilda Lessways* and Maupassant's *Une Vie* were the models for the episode in *Jerusalem the Golden* in which Clara reads through her dying mother's girlhood diaries.[4] The basic situation of *The Waterfall*—the protagonist's stealing her cousin's man—is reminiscent of *The Mill on the Floss*; both cousins are even named Lucy. In

The Realms of Gold the plot device that leads to the lovers' near-tragic misunderstanding—a quirk of fate causes the postcard Frances mails to her estranged lover, inviting a reconciliation, to get waylaid—is similar to the one Hardy used in *Tess of the D'Urbervilles*. And finally, *The Middle Ground* contains two episodes with distinct literary echoes: the scene in which Kate is flooded with acute childhood recollections as a result of sniffing the sewer smells that used to awe her as a child is, of course, based on Proust's similar experience with the madeleine cookie in *Remembrance of Things Past*, and the party scene that concludes the novel is quite clearly borrowed from *Mrs. Dalloway* (indeed, lest the unobservant reader miss the connection, Drabble mentions that it is Kate's daughter's reading of *Mrs. Dalloway* that gives her the idea of buying flowers for her party).

The theme of *The Millstone* is an ironic twist on that of *The Scarlet Letter*. Both stories are "moral fables" describing how the heroines pay for their sexual misconduct.[5] But Rosamund's "sin" is of a distinctly contemporary nature:

> My crime was my suspicion, my fear, my apprehensive terror of the very idea of sex. . . . I had the additional disadvantage of being unable to approve my own conduct; being a child of the age, I knew how wrong and how misguided it was. I walked around with a scarlet letter embroidered upon my bosom, . . . but the A stood for Abstinence, not for Adultery. In the end I even came to believe that I got it thus, my punishment [becoming pregnant as a result of her only sexual encounter], because I had dallied and hesitated and trembled for so long. (*Millstone*, pp. 21–22)

Drabble's handling of literary parallels is somewhat playful in this passage, but as Nancy Hardin argues, *The Millstone* can seriously be regarded as a "twentieth-century version of a moral fable. It is contemporary in its reliance on existential themes and on the burdens of choice falling on the individual, yet it resembles the earlier moral fable in that it can serve as an object lesson for young women of the present—a lesson in freedom as possibility."[6]

Hardin points out that *The Millstone* contains an additional literary echo: Samuel Daniel's sixteenth-century work *The Complaint of Rosamond* (Samuel Daniel is one of the poets Rosamund is writing her thesis on). Rosamund Stacey's first-person narrative resembles sixteenth-century complaint literature, a popular form whose purpose was to "enlighten the reader about the moral consequences of transgression against socially accepted codes of behavior."[7] But whereas Daniel's Rosamond must pay with her life, Drabble's heroine "confronts a moral dilemma whose quality is poignant. Neither death nor suicide nor even loss of self-esteem is possible for Rosamund of *The Millstone*. She acts so as to form a commitment to be within the world and, in that twentieth-century sense, pays for her transgression by opening herself to life."[8]

Besides specific literary themes, episodes, and characters, Drabble's novels also echo the general atmospheres of certain earlier works. The sublime, highly wrought passion that pervades the third-person sections of *The Waterfall* calls to mind the writing of the Brontës, to whom Drabble has been compared.[9] And the pervasive influence of Thomas Hardy can be seen in Drabble's acute awareness—most prominently displayed in *The Ice Age*—of the fickleness and ephemerality of good fortune.

But literary models do more than merely inform the structures and pervade the atmospheres of Drabble's novels. In addition, her protagonists turn to these models for guidance. Literature is a source of comfort for many of them. Emma's reading of Hume's views on marriage helps her to understand and accept her own difficult marriage, and a rereading of Wordsworth's early poems causes her to realize how much her sympathy has enlarged since her schooldays when she sniggered at these same works. Rosamund is better able to comprehend her irrational suspicion that her intense love for her infant daughter is what has caused the child to develop a critical illness by calling to mind Ben Jonson's poem to his dead son: "Ben Jonson said of his dead child, my sin was too much hope of thee, loved boy. We too easily take what the poets write as figures of speech, as pretty images as strings of *bons mots*. Sometimes perhaps they speak the truth" (*Millstone*, p. 141). Frances Wingate dispels gloomy thoughts of death by reflecting on how art can transform death into something beautiful; in particular, she recollects Gray's "Elegy." Similarly, reciting Milton's sonnet "On Blindness" enables her to endure the pain of childbirth and of a debilitating toothache. And Anthony Keating is saved from despair by reading *The Consolation of Philosophy*.

Literature also helps the characters comprehend the significance of their experiences. Frequently their thoughts turn to fictional analogues as a way of analyzing their own situations. When Sarah spends an unusual evening of intimacy with her ordinarily distant, difficult older sister, she is "struck as [they sit] there by the charming convention of the scene—sisters idling away an odd evening in happy companionship. It [is] like something out of *Middlemarch* or even Jane Austen" (*Bird-Cage*, p. 185). This perception, underscoring as it does the gap between appearance and reality, furthers the bitter education Sarah has been receiving about life and sharpens her sense of isolation. It also feeds her buried longing to have with Louise the kind of sisterly companionship portrayed in novels such as *Middlemarch* and *Pride and Prejudice*.

In *The Waterfall* Jane, in seeking to understand her tendency to be carried away by a grand passion, compares herself to literary models: "But love is nothing new. . . . It is a classic malady. . . . Perhaps I'll go mad with guilt, like Sue Bridehead, or drown myself in an effort to reclaim lost renunciations, like Maggie Tulliver. Those fictitious heroines, how they haunt me" (*Waterfall*, p. 184). Her ruminations lead her to the insight that although sexual mores have changed, women today still suffer as a result of love: "Maggie Tulliver never slept with her man: she did all the damage there was to be done, to Lucy, to herself, to the two men who loved her, and then, like a woman of another age, she refrained. In this age, what is to be done? We drown in the first chapter. I worry about the sexual doom of womanhood, its sad inheritance" (*Waterfall*, p. 184).

At another point Jane analyzes her response to Jane Austen's values as a way of gaining insight into her own abhorrence of middle-class respectability and her craving for passion:

> How I dislike Jane Austen. How deeply I deplore her desperate wit. Her moral tone dismays me: my heart goes out to the vulgarity of those little card parties that Mrs. Philips gave at Meryton, to that squalid rowdy hole at Portsmouth where Fanny Price used to live, to Lydia at fifteen gaily flashing her wedding ring through the carriage window, to Frank Churchill, above all to Frank Churchill, lying and deceiving and proffering embarassing extravagant gifts. Emma got what she deserved, in marrying Mr. Knightley. What can it have been like, in bed with Mr. Knightley? Sorrow awaited that woman: she would have done better to steal Frank Churchill, if she could. (*Waterfall*, pp. 65–66)

Still another example of how literature helps characters define their experiences is to be found in *Jerusalem the Golden*. Clara, baffled by the spectacle of sisterly affection she witnesses at the Denhams, a phenomenon hitherto unknown to her, suddenly can understand this type of relationship when she recollects Christina Rossetti's poem "Goblin Market": "she had always been strangely compelled by the passionate and erotic relationship described in the poem, so remote from any of the petty hostilities that she had ever witnessed. Descriptions and displays of passion had always compelled her, but she had considered this particular manifestation to be a fabrication, a convenient lie. She began to think that literature did not lie, after all; nothing was too strange to be true" (*Jerusalem*, p. 138).

Even children's fairy tales and moral fables can serve as sources of illumination for Drabble's characters. Emma's dilemma in an impossible social situation—she is trying simultaneously to please two guests with very different expectations of her behavior—causes her to recall "that fable, Aesop's no doubt, in which a boy and his father and a donkey set off on a journey and cannot satisfy any passer-by that they are rightly deployed" (*Garrick Year*, p. 99). The wisdom that Clara has imbibed from the story of the golden windows has already been mentioned. The same anthology that contains this story holds another called "The Two Weeds," whose moral ambivalence and suggestion that life involves open-ended choice has left a deep impression on Clara. Going against the tide of most moral fables, it hints that a life of "beauty and extravagance" (*Jerusalem*, p. 42), at the expense of judiciousness and moderation, is a possibility, and it is just such a daring approach to life that Clara has decided to take.

In *The Waterfall* the tale about the emperor's new clothes and another about a princess and a blue rose, both of whose themes have to do with the subjectivity of individual perception, provide Jane Gray with further speculation about her inability to see and record the truth accurately. A childhood fascination with *Pilgrim's Progress* helped develop in Rose Vassiliou the notion that her life would be a morally perilous journey. Finally, Kate Armstrong is deeply affected by a rereading of certain stories from *Old Peter's Russian Tales* that had fascinated her as a child. As her eyes fill with tears while reading "Alenoushka and Her Brother," she realizes that the story plays upon the complex emotional tie she has always felt to her own brother. Later, reflecting on how differently the life of an old school acquaintance has turned out from her sisters' lives, Kate is reminded of another Russian tale, "The Silver Saucer and the Transparent Apple," about "two wicked, greedy, vain, haughty, older sisters and a good, little, stupid one" (*Middle Ground*, p. 207). Although there is no obvious parallel between the three sisters of the tale and the three

Scott sisters, the story fires Kate's imagination and enables her to see the Scott girls' relationship in an archetypal framework.

Drabble's protagonists also have a penchant for musing on the nursery rhymes and verses they learned in childhood. Such apparently silly poems as those beginning "Mother, may I go out to swim" (*Garrick Year*, pp. 198–199), "Fudge, Fudge, Call the Judge" (*Needle's Eye*, p. 318), "Boatman, boatman, row my boat" (*Needle's Eye*, p. 135), and "For seven long years I served for you" (*Waterfall*, p. 239) can suddenly take on significance when pondered in the light of adult experience.[10] As Jane Campbell perceptively observes, "Margaret Drabble has seen that the imaginative apprehension of clichés can be an act of wisdom."[11]

But what are we to make, finally, of Drabble's heavy use of other literature in her novels? Bernard Bergonzi, citing Drabble's and other contemporary authors' tendencies in this direction, fears that it signals the decay of the novel: "Such borrowings and allusions have been commonplace throughout the ages in poetry and drama, forms which place less of a premium on originality, but to find them in the contemporary novel indicates that the form is losing its total commitment to originality and the immediate unique response to individual experience."[12]

Drabble's attachment to older literature, however, is not a form of parasitism; rather, it implies her belief that human beings cannot respond to experience in a totally free and original way. Our perceptions as well as our identities are shaped by a variety of forces, and the literature and myths of our culture constitute one of these. When Diana Cooper-Clark pointed out to Drabble in a recent interview that her "novels clearly echo with the literary heritage of England," the author responded, "Naturally, what I've read is as much a part of what I think as the people that I meet and the problems that I encounter. And when I find myself in what seems to me to be an unprecedented situation, I say to myself things such as, 'Now, what would so-and-so have written about this? What would their characters have felt in this situation?'. . . . It's very interesting to compare how characters in the past would have reacted. . . . So, I don't see it as decorating one's books with literature. I think that literature is a part of life."[13]

The relationship between literature and life is implicitly asserted in all Drabble's novels, by means of the various techniques surveyed above; but in three of her novels—*The Waterfall, The Realms of Gold,* and *The Middle Ground*—the author brings this relationship into the foreground. In *The Waterfall*, the most experimental of her works, she points out the intricate connection between art and life, in a fashion that reminds one of John Fowles, by having the protagonist narrate both a fictional and a nonfictional version of the same experience in an attempt to arrive at the truth of it. Jane is obsessed with the difficulty of perceiving and recording one's experience in an objective way, realizing that "the ways of regarding an event, so different, don't add up to a whole; they are mutually exclusive: the social view, the sexual view, the circumstantial view, the moral view" (*Waterfall*, p. 52). She would do well to add here "the literary view," for she reveals a propensity to regard her experience in a Brontësque light. In fact, at one point when reflecting on the way art and life overlap, she echoes Jane Eyre: "Reader, I loved him: as Charlotte Brontë said. Which was Charlotte Brontë's man, the one she created and wept for and longed for, or the poor curate that had her and killed her, her sexual measure, her sexual match?" (*Waterfall*, p. 99).

In *The Realms of Gold* and *The Middle Ground* Drabble uses a self-conscious, intrusive narrator who frequently comments on the act and art of creating the story. Whenever the narrator makes remarks such as "Invent a more suitable ending if you can" (*Realms*, p. 351), the narrative's realism is destroyed and we are made aware of the story as artifice. Although some readers complain about the jarring effect of this intrusion and find it out of place in otherwise realistic narratives, it does in fact contribute to one of Drabble's themes: the human need to give shape to raw experience by turning it into or seeing it in relation to a story.

Kate Armstrong, more than any of the other protagonists except perhaps Jane Gray, is acutely aware of this need. Coming from a drab, unhappy home, Kate early learned that even the dullest of situations can be transformed into something interesting by the power of words. She discovered a talent for amusing her friends with colorful anecdotes about her relatives: "out they all came, translated into art. It was like a kind of magic, turning shit into gold" (*Middle Ground*, p. 23). It was this fascination with "the gap between fantasy and reality" (*Middle Ground*, p. 25) that caused Kate to become a writer. Throughout the novel the protagonist and the narrator frequently speculate on how a situation can be arbitrarily cast in a particular light by the way it is reconstructed in words. What could just as easily be regarded as a dismal experience—for example, Kate's marriage to Stuart or the infidelities of her various friends—is made amusing by Kate's clever way with words.

In this novel Drabble additionally draws attention to the interplay between art and reality by including characters from her other works of fiction. As has already been pointed out, Rosamund Stacey and Gabriel and Phillipa Denhma are all invited to Kate's party. The reader familiar with Drabble's other novels recognizes these as "fictional" rather than "real" characters and thus the fictional nature of the story is underscored. But at the same time, the fact that these characters intermingle with the "real" people of the novel suggests the way literature and reality are intricately tied together.

Drabble's novels thus demonstrate the crucial role literature and story-telling play in human existence. Far from being parasitic or merely decorative, the literary echoes that abound in her fiction indicate the extent to which literature shapes our imaginations. In her interview with Barbara Milton, Drabble said that the purpose of literature is "to illumine what one sees in [the world],"[14] and to Nancy Hardin she described how it has personally helped her to do this:

> I find out about living and about the values of living—and a lot of my beliefs in life and my feelings about people and what to do—from reading novels. Very often I meet a kind of person that I'm not familiar with, which a novelist has given me a guideline on. I think novelists do that. They give you guidelines on familiar, unfamiliar people. You can feel much more sympathy with them because you've met them in a book before or encountered their backgrounds in a book.[15]

Margaret Drabble's belief in the importance of literature, especially the great literature of the past, points again to her essential traditionalism and conservatism. For her, the individual is not free: one's identity, perceptions, and actions are in good part shaped by forces beyond one's own will. The individual is intricately embedded in larger structures: fate, nature, and the family. Struggling against these demonstrates a misguided, immature approach to life; psychological and spiritual solace lies in submitting to them and in cherishing one's rich imaginative life.

In holding such views, Drabble is out of step with the intellectual and social climate that has prevailed throughout much of her writing career—a climate in which the individual and his or her freedoms are held up as the supreme value. While this trend has had its positive results, it has also given rise to a facile approach to the question of human happiness and well-being. Crash sessions of assertiveness-training and encounter-group therapy, for example, are expected to provide the individual with psychological freedom and enlightenment. This emphasis both on individual freedom and on easy answers goes very much against the grain of Drabble's thinking. Edith Milton, reviewing *The Ice Age*, suggests the important contribution Drabble makes to contemporary thought. She observes,

> People read very little Boethius these days, if, indeed, they ever heard of him, and he would be the last person to be surprised that researchers into the field of Happiness now bypass *The Consolation of Philosophy* to settle instead on *I'm O.K., You're O.K.* . . . [Boethius' book] became one of the great source books to comfort troubled souls in the Middle Ages and early Renaissance when they asked themselves why nothing seemed to work out the way it should.[16]

Edith Milton points out that although Boethius is largely forgotten today, now and again in Western thought "he still crops up," as he does in *The Ice Age*, which is pervaded with his philosophy.[17] Boethius, we remember, learned to submit gracefully to his fate—the curtailment of his freedom and worldly happiness as a result of undeserved imprisonment—by reminding himself that whatever happens to the individual has been willed by God and is for the good of the whole.

Both the matter and the manner of Boethius' reasoning appeal to Drabble. She too views the individual as a part of larger wholes, and she too advocates graceful acquiescence. It is a credit to her honesty and her courage that she voices views so unpopular today. Her body of fiction, which is not yet complete, presents a view of life rarely found in contemporary novels, one that is a welcome check against the existential tide.

Notes
Selected Bibliography
Index

Notes

1 Introduction

¹See, for example: "Woman's Mirror," rev. of *Jerusalem the Golden*, by Margaret Drabble, *Times Literary Supplement*, 13 Apr. 1967, p. 301; "Female and Male Subjects," rev. of *The Waterfall*, by Margaret Drabble, *Times Literary Supplement*, 22 May 1969, p. 549; Anthony Thwaite, rev. of *The Needle's Eye*, by Margaret Drabble, *New Statesman*, 31 Mar. 1972, p. 430; rev. of *The Needle's Eye*, by Margaret Drabble, *Choice*, Nov. 1972, pp. 1127–28; Lore Dickstein, rev. of *The Realms of Gold*, by Margaret Drabble, *New York Times Book Review*, 16 Nov. 1975, p. 5; David Hellerstein, "The Realms of Chance: An Encounter with Margaret Drabble," *Harvard Magazine*, Mar.–Apr. 1981, pp. 57–60.

²See, for example: Maureen Howard, rev. of *The Ice Age*, by Margaret Drabble, *New York Times Book Review*, 9 Oct. 1977, p. 7; Phyllis Rose, "Our Chronicler of Britain," rev. of *The Middle Ground*, by Margaret Drabble, *New York Times Book Review*, 14 Sept. 1980, pp. 1, 32–33.

³A. S. Byatt has published two novels, *The Game* and *The Virgin in the Garden*, and two scholarly works, *Degrees of Freedom: The Novels of Iris Murdoch* and *Wordsworth and Coleridge in Their Time*.

⁴All references to Drabble's novels will be to the first American editions (indicated in the list below) and will be cited parenthetically in the text, using the following short titles:

A Summer Bird-Cage (New York: Morrow, 1964)	*Bird-Cage*
The Garrick Year (New York: Morrow, 1965)	*Garrick Year*
The Millstone (New York: Morrow, 1966)	*Millstone*
Jerusalem the Golden (New York: Morrow, 1967)	*Jerusalem*
The Waterfall (New York: Knopf, 1969)	*Waterfall*
The Needle's Eye (New York: Knopf, 1972)	*Needle's Eye*
The Realms of Gold (New York: Knopf, 1975)	*Realms*
The Ice Age (New York: Knopf, 1977)	*Ice Age*
The Middle Ground (New York: Knopf, 1980)	*Middle Ground*

⁵Joan Manheimer, "Margaret Drabble and the Journey to the Self," *Studies in the Literary Imagination*, 11 (1978), 141.

⁶Nancy S. Hardin, "An Interview with Margaret Drabble," *Contemporary Literature*, 14 (1973), 290.

⁷Drabble made this comment to Bernard Bergonzi in one of his BBC interviews in the program series entitled "Novelists of the Sixties" (1967–68). The quote reap-

pears in Bergonzi's book *The Situation of the Novel* (London: Macmillan, 1970), p. 65.

[8] Walter Allen, rev. of *A Summer Bird-Cage*, by Margaret Drabble, *New Statesman*, 29 Mar. 1963, p. 466.

[9] "The Little Woman," rev. of *The Garrick Year*, by Margaret Drabble, *Times Literary Supplement*, 23 July 1964, p. 645.

[10] Rev. of *The Millstone*, by Margaret Drabble, *Library Journal*, 1 May 1966, p. 2361.

[11] Daniel Sterne, "What Emma Learned," rev. of *The Garrick Year*, by Margaret Drabble, *New York Times Book Review*, 4 Apr. 1965, p. 4.

[12] Stern, p. 4.

[13] Thwaite, p. 430.

[14] Letter to Mary Hurley Moran from John Curtis, 4 Sept. 1981.

[15] Virginia K. Beards, "Margaret Drabble: Novels of a Cautious Feminist," in *Contemporary Women Novelists: A Collection of Critical Essays*, ed. Patricia Meyer Spacks (Englewood Cliffs, N.J.: Prentice, 1977), p. 18. This article originally appeared in *Critique: Studies in Modern Fiction*, 15 (1973), 35–47.

[16] Elaine Showalter, *A Literature of Their Own: British Women Novelists from Brontë to Lessing* (Princeton: Princeton Univ. Pr., 1977), p. 304.

[17] Showalter, p. 305.

[18] Showalter, p. 306.

[19] Marion Vlastos Libby, "Fate and Feminism in the Novels of Margaret Drabble," *Contemporary Literature*, 16 (1975), 176.

[20] Showalter, p. 307.

[21] Showalter, p. 307.

[22] Manheimer, "Journey to the Self," pp. 127–28.

[23] Manheimer, "Journey to the Self," p. 142.

[24] Manheimer, "Journey to the Self," p. 142.

[25] Carey Kaplan, "A Vision of Power in Margaret Drabble's *The Realms of Gold*," *Journal of Women's Studies in Literature*, 4 (1978), 235.

[26] Kaplan, p. 242.

[27] Judy Little, "Humor and the Female Quest: Margaret Drabble's *The Realms of Gold*," *Regionalism and the Female Imagination*, 4 (Fall 1978), 8.

[28] Little, p. 4.

[29] Little, p. 8.

[30] Little, p. 8.

[31] Little, p. 8.

[32] See Drabble's remarks in her interview with Diana Cooper-Clark, "Margaret Drabble: Cautious Feminist," *Atlantic Monthly*, Nov. 1980, pp. 69–75.

[33] Bolivar Le Franc, "An Interest in Guilt," *Books and Bookmen*, 14 (Sept. 1969), 20.

[34] James Vinson, ed., *Contemporary Novelists* (New York: St. Martin's, 1972), p. 373.

[35] Mel Gussow, "Margaret Drabble: A Double Life," *New York Times Book Review*, 9 Oct. 1977, p. 7.

[36] See Drabble's remarks on this topic quoted in the following articles: Nancy Poland, "Margaret Drabble: 'There Must Be a Lot of People like Me,' " *Midwest Quarterly*, 16 (1975), 255–67; Ralph Tyler, "Margaret Drabble," *Bookviews*, Jan. 1978, pp. 7,9; Vinson, p. 373. Also see her discussion of how profoundly moved she was by her first reading of Simone de Beauvoir's *The Second Sex*, in her interview in Peter

Firchow, ed., *The Writer's Place: Interviews on the Literary Situation in Contemporary Britain* (Minneapolis: Univ. of Minnesota Pr., 1974), pp. 102–21.

[37] Margaret Drabble, "How Not To Be Afraid of Virginia Woolf," *Ms.*, Nov. 1972, pp. 68, 70, 72, 121.

[38] Drabble, like her protagonist Frances Wingate, successfully combines a time-consuming career (as writer, teacher, journalist, and editor) with the single-handed raising of a large family (she has three children and has been divorced for several years). She has always, even while married, supported herself, and she nearly sued a magazine which claimed she once observed that it is nice that married women can depend on their husbands' incomes and thereby have the leisure to write (see Poland, pp. 258–59).

[39] See the Cooper-Clark interview and Margaret Drabble, "Thinking About Rape," *New York Times*, 21 Jan. 1979, Sec. E, p. 21, cols. 2–3.

[40] Margaret Drabble, "The Author Comments," *Dutch Quarterly Review of Anglo-American Letters*, 5 (1975), 38.

[41] Margaret Drabble, Letter to Monica Lauritzen Manheimer, 26 Sept. 1974.

[42] In the Cooper-Clark interview, Drabble explains that *The Middle Ground* questions "whether feminism is still a good cause" (p. 75).

[43] Interestingly, Ellen Rose's reading of *The Waterfall* is at odds with the usual feminist reading, which criticizes Drabble for having Jane's salvation come about as a result of a love affair.

[44] Again, Ellen Rose differs from most feminist readers, who regard Frances Wingate as a stunning example of feminist achievement.

[45] Ellen Cronan Rose, *The Novels of Margaret Drabble: Equivocal Figures* (Totowa, N.J.: Barnes & Noble, 1980), p. 91.

[46] Rose, *The Novels of Margaret Drabble*, p. 129.

[47] François Bonfond, "Margaret Drabble: How to Express Subjective Truth Through Fiction," *Revue des Langues Vivantes*, 40 (1974), 50.

[48] Bonfond, p. 53.

[49] Nancy S. Hardin, "Drabble's *The Millstone*: A Fable for Our Times," *Critique: Studies in Modern Fiction*, 15 (1973), 25.

[50] Ellen Cronan Rose, "Margaret Drabble: Surviving the Future," *Critique: Studies in Modern Fiction*, 15 (1973), 16.

[51] In the conclusion to her book on Drabble, Ellen Rose explains the about-face she has done in her interpretation of the novels. Her thesis in the book being that Drabble's fiction contains a paradoxical double-message—both traditional humanist and (suppressed) radical feminist statements—she proves from her personal experience that a reader will perceive whichever message corroborates her own outlook at the time of the reading. When she first read Drabble in 1972, she was a bored, unhappy housewife, "frightened to admit the situation and guilty about it. What [she] saw in Drabble's novels was what this personal situation prepared [her] to see: self-denial, renunciation, an equation of womanhood with gritting one's teeth and bearing it" (p. 128). Now, however, after "a divorce, a Ph.D., a job at Dartmouth, the respect of [her] children, and the beginnings of a sense of self-esteem" (p. 128), when she reads Drabble she sees "what this book has just described. But while [she] now respond[s] primarily to the visionary message of her novels, [she] know[s]—from [her] own history more than from objective,

critical analysis—that the conservative message is still there, still being voiced, however inaudible it may be to women who hear, in *The Realms of Gold* for instance, a ringing affirmation of female autonomy" (pp. 128–29).

[52] Valerie Grosvenor Myer, *Margaret Drabble: Puritanism and Permissiveness*, Vision Critical Studies (London: Vision Press Limited, 1974), p. 15.

[53] Patricia Sharpe, "On First Looking into The Realms of Gold," *Michigan Quarterly Review*, 16 (1977), 225–31.

[54] Drabble, "The Author Comments," p. 36.

[55] Hardin, "An Interview," p. 283.

[56] Hardin, "An Interview," p. 289.

[57] Hardin, "An Interview," p. 284.

2 Drabble's Dark Universe

[1] See Drabble's comments about sin, guilt, retribution, and grace in her interviews with Terry Coleman ("Margaret Drabble Talks to Terry Coleman," *Manchester Guardian Daily*, 1 Apr. 1972, p. 8), Hardin, and Le Franc.

[2] In her interview with Hardin, Drabble remarked that she does not subscribe to any particular religious faith (p. 276) and said, "I'm really not quite sure what my theological position is" (p. 284).

[3] Margaret Drabble, *Arnold Bennett* (London: Weidenfeld and Nicolson, 1974), p. 13.

[4] See Hardin, "An Interview," p. 277; Le Franc, p. 21; and Gussow.

[5] John Marlowe, in *The Puritan Tradition in English Life* (London: The Cresset Press, 1956), explains, "Puritanism and Methodism were both based on an individual approach to God, without the intermediary of a priest. The Puritans sought to approach God through the Holy Spirit as revealed in Scripture, the Methodists through Jesus Christ as revealed to the human heart" (p. 45).
George M. Stephenson, in *The Puritan Heritage* (New York: MacMillan, 1952), observes, "The vitality of Puritanism was derived from a study of the Bible. It became the sole reading of the household" (p. 15).

[6] In Barbara Milton, "Margaret Drabble: The Art of Fiction LXX," *The Paris Review*, No. 74 (1978), Drabble states:

> What I'm perpetually trying to work out is the relationship between coincidence and plan. And in fact, I have this deep conviction that if you were to get high up enough over the world, you would see things that look like coincidence are, in fact, part of a pattern. This sounds very mystical and ridiculous, but I don't think it is. I think that I, in particular, and maybe certain other people have a need to perceive this pattern in coincidence. It may be that psychologically we're so afraid of the unpredictable, of the idea of chaos and disorder, that we wish to see order. (p. 62)

[7] Hardin, "An Interview," p. 284.

[8] John Updike, "Drabbling in the Mud," rev. of *The Realms of Gold*, by Margaret Drabble, *New Yorker*, 12 Jan. 1976, p. 88.

[9] In her interview with Barbara Milton, Drabble explained this view: "Take the fact that you should bump into somebody after ten years on your birthday after having last seen them at your birthday party. This is a coincidence, but it appears to have a meaning. We know it's superstitious, but so many times in my life I've had

coincidences like this that I'm driven to look for another underlying meaning" (p. 62).

[10]Le Franc, p. 21.

[11]Milton, "The Art of Fiction LXX," p. 48.

[12]Margaret Drabble, "Crossing the Alps," *Mademoiselle*, Feb. 1971, pp. 154–55, 193–98. Hereafter the title of this story will be shortened to "Alps" and references to it will be given in the text.

[13]Vinson, p. 373.

[14]Margaret Drabble, *Wordsworth*, Literature in Perspective (London: Evans Brothers Limited, 1966), p. 123.

[15]Margaret Drabble, "The Gifts of War," in *Winter's Tales*, 16, ed. A. D. MacLean (London: MacMillan, 1970), pp. 26–27. Hereafter the title of this story will be shortened to "Gifts" and references to it will be given in the text.

[16]Tyler, p. 7.

[17]Hardin, "An Interview," p. 282.

[18]Hardin, "An Interview," p. 282.

[19]For particular examples of humor in *The Realms of Gold*, see Little's article.

[20]Milton, "The Art of Fiction LXX," p. 57.

3 Nature and the Individual

[1]Margaret Drabble, *A Writer's Britain: Landscape in Literature* (New York: Knopf, 1979), p. 40.

[2]Milton, "The Art of Fiction LXX," p. 44.

[3]In the Cooper-Clark interview Drabble explained that in part *The Middle Ground* is "about one's children growing up": "My children are all teenagers now, and it's hilarious but ghastly. I've dedicated it to my daughter, because I use quite a lot of copy from her. It's about being a mother to teenage children and knowing that the children are going to be gone any minute now. And you've done all the things in your life you meant to do—what next? She knows there's something next and she doesn't know what it is" (p. 75).

[4]Margaret Drabble, "Hardy and the Natural World," in *The Genius of Thomas Hardy*, ed. Margaret Drabble (London: Weidenfeld and Nicolson, 1976), p. 164.

[5]Drabble, "Hardy and the Natural World," p. 165.

[6]Drabble, "Hardy and the Natural World," pp. 164–65.

[7]Updike, p. 90.

[8]Drabble, *A Writer's Britain*, p. 161.

[9]John Alcorn, *The Nature Novel from Hardy to Lawrence* (New York: Columbia Univ. Pr., 1977), p. 6.

[10]Myer, p. 110.

[11]Drabble, *Arnold Bennett*, pp. 119–20.

[12]Robert Langbaum, *The Mysteries of Identity: A Theme in Modern Literature* (New York: Oxford Univ. Pr., 1977).

4 Family and the Individual

[1]Milton, "The Art of Fiction LXX," p. 56.

[2]In Dee Preussner, "Talking with Margaret Drabble," *Modern Fiction Studies*, 25

(1979–80), Drabble discusses her own urge to move back to the region her ancestors came from, remarking, "there's something [strong] that wants to go somewhere where the family came from" (p. 573).

[3] Gaston Bachelard, *The Poetics of Space*, trans. Maria Jolas (Boston: Beacon Pr., 1969), p. 78.

[4] Milton, "The Art of Fiction LXX," p. 54.

[5] A. S. Byatt, *The Game* (London: Chatto & Windus, 1967).

[6] In her interview with Preussner, Drabble said, "I feel a great confidence in the family situation that comes through whether I want it to or not" (p. 569).

[7] Northrop Frye, *Anatomy of Criticism: Four Essays* (Princeton: Princeton Univ. Pr., 1957).

[8] See Drabble's comment about the family today being what one chooses to make it (Preussner, p. 569).

[9] Drabble, "The Author Comments," p. 38.

5 Imagination: The Role of Vision

[1] Milton, "The Art of Fiction LXX," p. 62. See also Drabble's comments on her belief in fate and a divine plan in Hardin, "An Interview," pp. 14, 213.

[2] Milton, "The Art of Fiction LXX," p. 63.

[3] Margaret Drabble, "A Voyage to Cythera," *Mademoiselle*, Dec. 1967, p. 150. Hereafter the title of this story will be shortened to "Voyage" and references to it will be given in the text.

[4] Hardin, "An Interview," p. 293.

[5] This story was published as "The Reunion" in *Winter's Tales*, 14, ed. Kevin Crossley-Holland (London: Macmillan, 1968), pp. 149–68, and as "Faithful Lovers" in *Saturday Evening Post*, 6 Apr. 1968, pp. 52–65. All further references will be to "Reunion" and will be given in the text.

[6] Hardin, "An Interview," p. 277.

[7] Rose, "Surviving the Future," p. 16.

[8] Rose, "Surviving the Future," p. 14.

[9] Margaret Drabble, "Hassan's Tower," in *Winter's Tales*, 12, ed. A.D. MacLean (London: Macmillan, 1966), pp. 57–58.

[10] Hardin, "An Interview," p. 284.

[11] Coleman, p. 8.

[12] Hardin, "An Interview," p. 27.

[13] Drabble, "The Author Comments," p. 35.

6 Imagination: The Role of Literature

[1] For a fuller survey of Drabble's use of literary echoes, see Jane Campbell, "Margaret Drabble and the Search for Analogy," in *The Practical Vision: Essays in Honour of Flora Roy*, ed. Jane Campbell and James Doyle (Waterloo, Ontario: Wilfrid Laurier Univ. Pr., 1978), pp. 133–50. I am indebted to Ms. Campbell for pointing out a few literary allusions that I missed.

[2] I am indebted to Virginia K. Beards for the information about the source of the title of *A Summer Bird-Cage* ("Margaret Drabble: Novels of a Cautious Feminist," p.

20). I have already cited the Biblical lines to which the title *The Needle's Eye* alludes. I am indebted to Nancy S. Hardin for the information that the title *The Millstone* alludes to the verse in Matthew 18:6, "Whoso shall offend one of these little ones which believe in me, it were better that a millstone were hanged about his neck, and that he were drowned in the depth of the sea" ("An Interview," p. 280).

[3] Bergonzi, p. 22.

[4] Bergonzi, p. 22.

[5] Rosamund Stacey points out that her experience would serve as a "moral fable for young women" (*Millstone*, p. 20).

[6] Hardin, "Drabble's *The Millstone*," p. 25.

[7] Hardin, "Drabble's *The Millstone*," p. 27.

[8] Hardin, "Drabble's *The Millstone*," pp. 27–28.

[9] Poland, p. 255. In her article "The Writer as Recluse: The Theme of Solitude in the Works of the Brontës," in *Brontë Society Transactions*, 16 (1974), 259–69, Drabble discusses the similarity between her childhood and the Brontës'.

[10] Ellen Cronan Rose thinks that a symbolic feminist message is suddenly perceived by Emma in the children's rhyme, "Mother, may I go out to swim": "Don't go near the water, don't get wet 'with milk and blood and tears, a varied sea of grief' (*Garrick Year*, p. 190), with the wetness that is the essence of female sexuality—the blood of menstruation, the lubricity of the ready vagina, the broken sac of amniotic fluid" (*The Novels of Margaret Drabble*, p. 14).

[11] Campbell, p. 139.

[12] Bergonzi, pp. 22–23.

[13] Cooper-Clark, p. 71.

[14] Milton, "The Art of Fiction LXX," p. 59.

[15] Hardin, "An Interview," p. 279.

[16] Edith Milton, rev. of *The Ice Age*, by Margaret Drabble, *The New Republic*, 22 Oct. 1977, p. 28.

[17] Milton, rev. of *The Ice Age*, p. 28.

Selected Bibliography
of Drabble's Works

I. Books

Novels

The Garrick Year. London: Weidenfeld and Nicolson, 1964; New York: Morrow, 1965.

The Ice Age. London: Weidenfeld and Nicolson, 1977; New York: Knopf, 1977.

Jerusalem the Golden. London: Weidenfeld and Nicolson, 1967; New York: Morrow, 1967.

The Middle Ground. London: Weidenfeld and Nicolson, 1980; New York: Knopf, 1980.

The Millstone. London: Weidenfeld and Nicolson, 1965; New York: Morrow, 1966; rpt. as *Thank You All Very Much*. New York: New American Library, 1969.

The Needle's Eye. London: Weidenfeld and Nicolson, 1972; New York: Knopf, 1972.

The Realms of Gold. London: Weidenfeld and Nicolson, 1975; New York: Knopf, 1975.

A Summer Bird-Cage. London: Weidenfeld and Nicolson, 1962; New York: Morrow, 1964.

The Waterfall. London: Weidenfeld and Nicolson, 1969; New York: Knopf, 1969.

Nonfiction

Arnold Bennett. London: Weidenfeld and Nicolson, 1974.

For Queen and Country: Britain in the Victorian Age. New York: Seabury Pr., 1979.

Wordsworth. Literature in Perspective. London: Evans Brothers Limited, 1966.

A Writer's Britain: Landscape in Literature. New York: Knopf, 1979.

Editions

ed. *The Genius of Thomas Hardy*. London: Weidenfeld and Nicolson, 1976.

ed. *Lady Susan, The Watsons, Sanditon*. By Jane Austen. London: Penguin, 1974.

and B. S. Johnson, eds. *London Consequences*. London: Greater London Arts Association, 1972.

II. Short Stories

"Crossing the Alps." *Mademoiselle*, Feb. 1971, pp. 154–55, 193–98.

"Day in the Life of a Smiling Woman, A." in *In the Looking Glass: Twenty-One Modern Short Stories by Women*. Ed. Nancy Dean and Myra Stark. New York: Putnam, 1977.

"Faithful Lovers." *Saturday Evening Post*, 6 April 1968, pp. 52–65. Also published as "The Reunion."

"Gifts of War, The." In *Winter's Tales*, 16. Ed. A. D. MacLean. London: Macmillan, 1970, pp. 20–36.

"Hassan's Tower." In *Winter's Tales*, 12. Ed. A. D. MacLean. London: Macmillan, 1966, pp. 41–59.

"Homework." *The Ontario Review*, Fall–Winter 1977–78, pp. 7–13.

"Reunion, The." In *Winter's Tales*, 14. Ed. Kevin Crossley-Holland. London: Macmillan, 1968, pp. 149–68. Also published as "Faithful Lovers."

"Success Story, A." *Ms.*, Dec. 1974, pp. 52, 54–55, 94.

"Voyage to Cythera, A." *Mademoiselle*, Dec. 1967, pp. 98–99, 148–50.

III. Selected Articles and Reviews

"Author Comments, The" *Dutch Quarterly Review of Anglo-American Letters*, 5 (1975), 35–38.

"Cassandra in a World Under Siege." *Ramparts*, Feb. 1972, pp. 50–54.

"Fearful Fame of Arnold Bennett, The" *Observer*, 11 May 1967, pp. 12–14.

"Hardy and the Natural World." In *The Genius of Thomas Hardy*. Ed. Margaret Drabble. London: Weidenfeld and Nicolson, 1976, pp. 162–69.

"How Not To Be Afraid of Virginia Woolf." *Ms.*, Nov. 1972, pp. 68, 70, 72, 121.

"Jane Fonda: Her Own Woman at Last?" *Ms.*, Oct. 1977, pp. 51–53, 88–89.

"Revelations and Prophecies." *Saturday Review*, 27 May 1978, pp. 54, 56.

"Thinking About Rape." *New York Times*, 21 Jan. 1979, Sec. E, p. 21, cols. 2–3.

"Woman Writer, A." *Books*, No. 11 (Spring 1973), pp. 4–6.

"Writer as Recluse: The Theme of Solitude in the Works of the Brontës, The." In *Brontë Society Transactions*, 16 (1974), 259–69.

Index